What you hold in your hands is 61 years of knowledge, experience and the wisdom that Joe, a man who has hit rock bottom several times found and is so openly sharing.

Joe always knew that there was more and that there was another way. His desire to uncover the truths of life, what is so readily available to all of us, and his innate desire to help others is evident in his words and wisdoms.

As you turn each page my wish for you is that a new truth finds it's home within your heart and may you go out and live by example.

With love and blessings

Joanne Antoun

* Joanne Antoun is a Lecturer in the field of Personal Growth and Consciousness, a Gifted Medium, Creator and trainer of <u>CTC Technique</u>, a Psychotherapist, <u>Reiki Master Teacher</u>, <u>NLP Master Practitioner</u> and Trainer, Hypnotherapy Trainer, <u>EFT Trainer</u>, Life Coach, Inspirational Speaker, Teacher of Accelerated Learning Techniques, and an Author.

Joanne is available for Corporate Events.

Joanne is now <u>personally training students</u> to deliver her incredibly transformative 2 hour CTC—Combined Therapy Cocktail session.

What if
YOU
ARE YOUR
GOD?

WHAT'S THE BOOK ABOUT?

IT'S A "REPAIR" MANUAL,
FOR YOUR LIFE.

What if
YOU
ARE YOUR
GOD?

ARE YOU IN CONTROL OF YOUR LIFE?

EMIDDIO JOE CATALDO

BALBOA.
PRESS

A DIVISION OF HAY HOUSE

Balboa Press books may be ordered through booksellers or by contacting:

Balboa Press
A Division of Hay House
1663 Liberty Drive
Bloomington, IN 47403
www.balboapress.com.au
1-(877) 407-4847

ISBN: 978-1-4525-1103-0 (sc)
ISBN: 978-1-4525-1104-7 (e)

Because of the dynamic nature of the Internet, any web addresses or links contained in this book may have changed since publication and may no longer be valid. The views expressed in this work are solely those of the author and do not necessarily reflect the views of the publisher, and the publisher hereby disclaims any responsibility for them.

The author of this book does not dispense medical advice or prescribe the use of any technique as a form of treatment for physical, emotional, or medical problems without the advice of a physician, either directly or indirectly. The intent of the author is only to offer information of a general nature to help you in your quest for emotional and spiritual well-being. In the event you use any of the information in this book for yourself, which is your constitutional right, the author and the publisher assume no responsibility for your actions.

Any people depicted in stock imagery provided by Thinkstock are models, and such images are being used for illustrative purposes only. Certain stock imagery © Thinkstock.

Printed in the United States of America

Balboa Press rev. date: 08/14/2013

THIS IS YOUR LIFE, RIGHT NOW; THIS MOMENT.

HOW ARE YOU DOING?

IS EVERYTHING WORKING OUT?

REALY EVERYTHING, ALL ASPECTS?

IT'S TAKEN OVER SIXTY YEARS OF PRACTICE, AND I AM STILL LEARNING NEW AND EXCITING METHODS TO IMPROVE MY OWN LIFE.

CURRENTLY, I'M PRACTICING MEDITATION, YOGA, TI-CHI, QI-GONG, HYPNOSIS, EFT, MASSAGE, REFLEXOLOGY AS WELL AS MANY OTHER SELF IMPROVEMENT MODALITIES THAT I HAVE INCORPORATED INTO MY EVERYDAY WAY OF LIFE.

WHAT ARE YOU DOING?

Two famous quotes, by Albert EINSTIEN, are so true for me and my life, I will share them here.

"Two things are infinite; the universe and human stupidity; and, I am not sure about the universe."

And the other is:-

"There are only two ways to live your life. One is as though nothing is a miracle; the other is as though everything is a miracle."

Your world, is exactly that; your world.

Change your perceptions, the way you view this world, change your thoughts, and your world will change. It has to follow the simple rule of reflecting back to you whatever you are focused on. This law of attracting what we focus on is so simple, yet widely miss understood.

DO YOU EVER FEEL:-

HELPLESS?

POWERLESS?

THAT EVERYTHING IS STACKED AGAINST YOU?

THAT YOU ARE NOT IN CONTROL?

OVERWHELMED BY EVENTS?

AT A LOSS AS TO EXPLAIN WHY?

ANGRY WITH OTHERS?

AFRAID OF WHAT LIES AHEAD?

IF YOU ANSWERED YES TO ANY OF THE ABOVE QUESTIONS THEN THIS BOOK IS FOR YOU!

CONTENTS

Dedication.. xvii
Introduction.. xxi
Preface... xxv

Chapter 1   Expect and Respect Differences................................... 1
Chapter 2   Who are You? Where are You?
             What Do You Want To Be When You Grow Up?............ 7
Chapter 3   Understanding Feelings or
             Negative Energy / Positive Energy............................... 17
Chapter 4   What Seeds are You Sowing?...................................... 25
Chapter 5   How Can We Change?... 31
Chapter 6   Ultimate Power to Recreate Your World Now 35
Chapter 7   Relationships... 39
Chapter 8   Love.. 47
Chapter 9   Are You Living for Yesterday, Today, or Tomorrow?..... 49
Chapter 10   Anger.. 51
Chapter 11   All Problems are Opportunities.................................... 57
Chapter 12   How Our Emotions Affect Our Health......................... 61
Chapter 13   Forgiveness... 63
Chapter 14   A Simplified Version of The Spirit World 65
Chapter 15   Distorted Thought 67

Personal Testimony... 75
Conclusion 81
Summary... 83
Appendix... 85

TAKE CONTROL
of
YOUR
LIFE FORCE / SOURCE ENERGY / GOD

The mind-body-spirit connection has to be viewed as one life force running through each of us. Often we tend to overlook the obvious!

In 2012 scientists conducted an experiment which actually proved the existence of what has been termed "THE GOD PARTICLE".

This particle was discovered many years ago, however technology has now caught up with theory, and science has proof that within every atom, there exists this particle. Every atom, imagine that.

Everything that is seen and un-seen, absolutely all things, including every one of the estimated 50 trillion cells in our bodies, contains this GOD particle.

Imagine, for just a moment, taking charge of this particle that is within you.

Imagine if this particle was totally in-sync with every part of your body.

Imagine when you get together with other people with similar "particles" that are in-sync with yours. For instance, at a sporting event, a concert, a cinema, or a church, the energy that is generated within each individual is multiplied and amplified. You can actually feel it.

Just as the ocean is made up of water, un-calculable quantities of tiny drops, you cannot separate the ocean from each drop.

The energy / source within each of our now over 7 billion human population, contains this similar characteristic. We are part of the whole. Each one of us, as individuals, contain within us, the same composition as others.

This power, this energy, this life force, within each of us, is what this book is about. Modern western teaching, however disregards this force, and usually, when illness strikes, concentrates on drugs intended to give instant results, treating the symptoms, not the cause.

If, instead, we search within, we will discover the cause, and thereby eliminating pain and suffering, as treating symptoms alone, cannot.

Imagine a sensor that picked up signals / frequencies, from all sources and instantly analyzed and responded appropriately.

Imagine this sensor is within you, however no-one gave you an instruction manual.

Imagine that. A powerful device designed to connect with any and every conceivable frequency in the galaxy and no instructions on how to make optimum use of this device.

Imagine using only sight, hearing, smell, touch, and voice, when there are a multitude of other senses included at no charge. Is there a sixth sense, or are there even more?

Our body is equipped with precision instrumentation to analyze SENSATIONS, VIBRATIONS, FREQUENCIES, FROM ALL SOURCES, EACH AND EVERY MOMENT.

Our estimated 50 trillion cells communicate with each other every instant. Our energy radiates into our surroundings, much similar to the ripples generated by a stone dropped into water.

Most of us are simply not aware of this. It goes un-noticed, out of sight, out of mind.

Today, these frequencies are measured with very sensitive electronic equipment, namely the EEG and ECG, as well as MRI and CAT scans.

What if, we could finally discover a user manual that would allow us to learn how to make better use of our equipment, namely our body, mind and spirit?

The possibilities are infinite. We would be able to read these frequencies and detect blockages or interferences as they occur. This may defeat "dis-ease" and illness, from our bodies.

What if, alternative medicine, energy medicine, natural medicine, is doing this already?

The following are just a few of the alternative fields of healing practices available today.

Acupuncture. Aromatherapy. Chiropractic. Color therapy. Herbal medicine. Homeopathy. Holistic medicine. Counseling therapies. Emotional Field Therapy. Spiritual healing. Neural Linguistic Programming. Faith healing. Kinesiology. Hypnosis. Magnetic therapy. Salt therapy. Mineral therapy. Mineral baths. Oxygen therapy. The list goes on, and on.

Our untapped potential could solve all our problems of ill health and possibly more.

What would our bodies be like if they could be completely disease free by simply eating healthy foods?

What if our bodies co-operated and worked with Mother Nature and our planet Earth?

What if all humans could co-exist in harmony with Mother Nature and each other?

Imagine a world in harmony, global peace and tranquility. Imagine co-operation between all peoples, sharing resources including food, with others.

Imagine living from our HEART, with love for all living things.

What if Hypocrites was correct in saying "LET YOUR FOOD BE YOUR MEDICINE"?

What if you ate unprocessed, unrefined, organic foods picked fresh and full of vital, life sustaining energy?

DEDICATION

I dedicate this book to all the free spirits in the universe, especially those that are troubled by their way of living their life or, by the way they react to the events in their life. This usually manifests itself in our bodies by causing pain and suffering. This pain and suffering is not restricted to our non physical area, which includes depression, fear, mood disorders and the like, but also pain in our physical body. If you want to achieve a healthy body, mind, and spirit, you must learn how this connection works.

Once this understanding is made, anything you focus your mind on will eventuate for you.

Unfortunately the majority of people never take the time to examine their life. They are always too busy just living. They are not expert in their finances, so they go to the so-called advisors, who get paid by a boss just like they do. They are not expert in their health, so they go to doctors to treat their symptoms of their illness / disease, usually by a drug or other substance manufactured for profit. Why could our life not be simplified?

Why not make the connection between three controlling forces in our bodies? In fact you could even class them with the controlling laws of our universe, or Mother Nature.

Our bodies are a magnificent piece of work designed by a higher power of the universe.

I will refer to GOD in this book. For those who do not believe in a GOD, I simply ask you to put another "O" in this word so it reads GOOD. And you can call this the balance of good over evil. This is NOT a religious book, but it is an attempt to draw on my knowledge of how the mind, body, spirit, connection works in every one of us.

It was not until I met a dear friend, Dr. BRIAN COSTELLO, just a few years ago, he literally took me under his wing. I was 150 kg, had very high blood pressure, high cholesterol, and type-2 diabetes, among other things. He was instrumental in turning my life around. I now weigh 115kg, have better blood pressure than my GP, and my diabetes and cholesterol levels are within healthy parameters, and all of this has come about without medication.

The exercise routines are secondary to the relaxation / meditation methods employed. Any form of physical activity will burn calories. When combined with the correct mental focus, a powerful energy is engaged. What I have learnt about this power, this energy, this force, I have put down on paper. I am by no means an expert, but I have absorbed information related to the mind, and how it works for over half a century. There are many books, tapes, CD's, courses, seminars, and therapists that have contributed to my knowledge of the mind, and how our behavior is associated directly to it.

Our actions are all LEARNT; as such they can be UN-LEARNT.

Take what works for you from this information. What doesn't, ignore it, but give it a go at least. You have nothing to lose.

Professor R. H. Brian Costello
PhD FCP (Lond) Dip FAB Med Psych Dip ABPs Dip ABFE FAAIM FACFE MACE

Forensic Examiner, Neuropsychologist and Clinical Psychologist
Ambassador for the International Council of Psychologists, Est 1943
Eminent Fellow of Wisdom, National Hall of Fame, Beverly Hills

27-October-2003

Dear Joe

Thank you for your two recent letters and especially the thoughtfulness and kindness of what you so eloquently expressed. My work now is caught up in research with very tight deadlines here and overseas so truly I simply am not available apart from seeing only a few patients.

Your idea of making physical fitness and psychological wellbeing a practical program is as we both know, not a new concept. However the enthusiasm and original approach you envisage appears innovative in a different way because of your own personal success in weight reduction and greatly improved fitness.

Concerning your dear father, of course I think of you both still and the wonderful chats we had together by the walnut tree. Although on the surface what we achieved could have appeared miraculous, basically it was an application of Mind-Body Medicine. He had a definite purpose to live longer and the faith to achieve it against all odds. For my part it was several applications of restoring his self-concept and helping him transfer his thoughts into action. We all did this together, with him to defeat temporarily what was although inevitable. A touch of powerful loving sensitivity on the family's part, large dose of humour and probably one of the stronger ingredients was his distraction from pain and fear. His belief in miracles like the mystic Padre Pio and others worked for him in a Christ-like way.

All the very best dear Joe in what you are doing with GROW and also for the company you have formed where hopefully you will help people achieve so much through positive attitude, physical fitness and good nutrition. When people have faith and hope possibly the only ingredient forgotten is "charity" so with that in mind, maybe this can be gleaned in a different way rather than just financial donation and preferably in just helping others who need help. You and GROW group members already understand this concept perfectly well, of course.

Yours sincerely,

"The Ibis Lodge" PO Box 1114 Pearcedale, AUSTRALIA 3912
Tel +61 359 786 888 Fax +61 359 787 323 Email: bcos5371@bigpond.net.au
www.cassel.edu.au and www.icimedicine.com

INTRODUCTION

This book is based on my interpretations of the events, in my life, that have caused me to become the person I am today. My beliefs, my values, my code of ethics / practice, my standards, my understanding of the knowledge I have gained along life's journey.

Sometimes I know only too well that some people think that I'm crazy. All I can respond to this notion is by repeating a famous saying from the Tuscany region of Italy, roughly translated to the following. "We are all from the same root, some a little more twisted than others."

The purpose of this book was originally to help one person in my life, the one that was so dear and special, that I would give my world to. But as always, when you start something new, you always find new events unfolding before your very eyes. My God really works in mysterious ways.

I started to entertain the thought that if I could only help this person to view things differently, possibly this person could see things my way.

And then as I typed this manuscript, and put pen to paper, so to speak, more like pushing the buttons on my keyboard, one at a time, using one finger at a time, it came to me that I was limiting my help to only one person. My love of people in general, kicked in, and I started to dream about the wider population. What if I could impart this information to the whole of humanity?

I have started something that I believe will help everyone who is prepared to examine their individual lives, and if they can empower themselves with the information herein, then I will have served my purpose.

Many of you will not accept what I have to say, and that's ok, I respect your right to choose.

Enjoy your journey through life, and I sincerely wish you well in all your pursuits, in whatever area of your life that you need to improve I simply ask you to remember the following . . .

There is only one thing that is absolutely certain . . . and that is death; we only make everything else in our life certain by the meanings / significance, we attach to them.

We create for ourselves, by our perceptions, our interpretations, our power of reasoning, our judgment, assumptions, convictions, etc. the world we choose to live in.

This inner world is the realm in which this book concentrates its' focus. Hopefully the reader will gain some insight into their own inner workings of their mind in order that they too can learn how to control their thoughts, emotions, and reactions to all the events that unfold before them, as they travel along their journey through life.

Along the way, this book also attempts to explain the MIND, BODY, SPIRIT connection that exists within each of us. As we all know, in theory at least, the body has a brain that controls all of our bodily functions that we know of and then some that we are yet to discover. Our spirit or soul is also present, even if we cannot see it.

The best way to explain this possibly is to draw an analogy between our cars of today and our bodies. Our car has a power plant, the motor, which is connected to a transmission or gearbox, which is connected via the drive train to the wheels. Together with various systems to make everything operate the way it should. Today, in fact, there are systems in place to compensate for our mistakes e.g. air bags, ABS, EFI, the list goes on. Our bodies have their power plant, which is our physical body. Our bodies have various systems, the nervous system, skeletal system, respiratory system to name just a few. Our bodies also have a DRIVER. This is the one behind the wheel, the one making all the decisions, choices, the pilot in CONTROL. This is where spirit comes in.

In fact you could say the spirit is like the fuel you feed your car. If you give it the correct fuel, it performs well. If on the other hand you put adulterated fuel in, it plays up or doesn't go at all. It could even break down completely to the point you need to replace bits and pieces of your car.

I know this analogy is rather crude, but if you think about it you will get my idea of this connection that exists between our bodies, and our spirit that is controlling our mind. Whether you accept this or not is irrelevant, because our bodies were designed by a form of intelligence or power far greater than all of us put together. Modern science has yet to unravel the complexities of our human bodies let alone our mind. By reading the following pages, I am sure this connection between the mind and spirit will become clearer to you. I sincerely hope it does.

Recently I attended a series of seminars by Dr. Bruce H. LIPTON, a leading cellular biologist and renowned author of several books, his latest "Spontaneous Evolution", explains how the emerging new science of EPIGENETICS, has discovered that our cells contained in our DNA actually interact with signals from our environment. This is completely mind blowing, as all our former beliefs are stuck in the old sciences which are being challenged and proved to be based on false assumptions. Our genes are controlled by the environment we create within our own bodies, as well as the world around us.

One final note, for our bodies to perform at their best, we need to know something else which is critical in this connection issue. All our bodies systems work on chemistry. That is how our cells communicate throughout our bodies via an electrical magnetic / chemical transmission. Each atom has negative or positive ions. This is what allows the flow of all the various molecules, neurons, oxygen, blood, hormones, and nutrients, etc. That is why we must be very careful of the negative energies we are creating within our bodies from time to time. As you will see, this negative energy can and does upset the delicate balance that we need to maintain for optimum health.

This electrical magnetic / chemical energy is all around us today more than ever. We know of various studies worldwide, that have alerted us to possible dangers of being exposed to high-tension electric cables, and also various levels of EMR coming from electrical devices, such as mobile phones and computers. We must be mindful of the possible interference with our own bodies functioning when exposed to these elements, needless to mention the chemicals that abound in our environment.

PREFACE

WHY DO WE DO WHAT WE DO?

Have you ever stopped to think why we do the things we do? Have you ever wondered what it's all about? Have you found a purpose for your being? Have you thought about why are you here; what is your aim, your goal? How much time do we have left to achieve the things we want to achieve? These and many other questions are necessary to answer in our lifetime.

What drives you in life is what gets you out of bed in the morning, makes you stay up late at night. The thing that directs your focus will pull you toward that goal. Each one of us has our own DRIVE, for the most part each is different, and yet the same.

There must be some higher purpose for your existence than just being on the treadmill. Getting up, going to work, going to bed, just to repeat the process the next day and the next, and the next.

Everything in life has a purpose, including you. Our creator, GOD if you like, doesn't make junk. All of us were put here for a purpose. It is up to each one of us to seek out what that is. We can direct our focus on any purpose we wish to. The secret is to choose what your purpose is, at least for the moment, and go for it. You may choose other purposes along the way, but essentially the main driving force directing you, will be the same.

We must look for something that transcends our own self, something that is eternal. A higher purpose than merely our own individual needs and wants. This purpose usually is not a material one but rather an intangible sense of what we are about as human beings. This could be a sense of service, of caring, of giving, of loving, of dedication, of looking after your body, your health, your soul, as well as many others. This purpose for our life will be different for each of us, and yet it will be the same.

When you discover what this higher purpose is for you, you will always have that purpose available to you even during the darkest moments. Even when things go horribly wrong, you will find strength through this purpose. This overall purpose for your existence will never falter. It may alter slightly, but essentially it will remain the same. To give you an example, you may find the following useful. Let's say your purpose was to serve fellow man, to love and be loved, to respect life in whatever form, to be happy and enjoy life. If in the future, you add something like "my purpose is to have a good time", you can see this fits in with being happy and enjoying life, that's fine. There are no contradictions.

It is my belief that it is when you have contradictions in your purpose, and your behavior, that you cause problems in your life.

WHAT TYPE OF PERSON ARE YOU?

I am sure you have all heard the following, "there are those who want it to happen, those who let it happen, and those who make it happen", or variations, those who make it happen, those who let it happen, and those who ask what's happened.

The type who want it to happen, include people who go around thinking that it would be nice if one day. They should do this, or they could do that. They are forever telling themselves stories about what would be nice, or worse still, what is rotten in their life

This category include the thinkers, and those forever whining and complaining about life, and wanting it to improve, but not doing anything to implement change.

The next group who let it happen, are those who believe that their life is "normal", and just go with the flow, as it were. They are content to just exist, and believe that they are powerless to do any better. If only they had enough money, or they were dealt a stroke of good luck. If only. If only. This category, firmly believe that life is preordained, and they just have to grin and bear it. They were born unlucky, or their parents were poor, or whatever other story you wish to make up.

The last group, are those who make it happen, the achievers, the leaders in their fields. These people make up their minds, and take appropriate action, and obtain results. Their reality is the belief that they can get results, they can plan their steps, and they can achieve their goals. They take responsibility for their own life. They have their eye on their goal and just get on with it, no matter how many times they fall; they just pick themselves up and keep going.

YOUR **BELIEFS** INFLUENCE YOUR **THOUGHTS** WHICH EFFECT YOUR **VIEWS / PERCEPTIONS** WHICH DICTATE YOUR **BEHAVIOUR** (THOUGHTS / WORDS / ACTIONS)

If you are behaving in a particular manner, you have a belief in place, which does NOT allow you to act any other way. If you get upset / angry, over certain things, you may have a belief which has been violated in some way.

Allow me to illustrate:-

Imagine you have a belief that goes something like this; "I respect my property, I look after it, it will last a long time".

This belief causes you to do things such as clean and maintain your "property", i.e., all your possessions, meticulously. This belief also causes great pain and suffering and possibly anger, when you find your "property" NOT clean or perfect, especially when other people are involved who do not share your belief-e.g.—Your partner, neighbors, work mates, friends etc.

In order to conduct a form of self-analysis, you need to investigate the validity of each of your beliefs that may be causing you to react the way you do. The way one does this is to identify the BASIC NEED you have which this belief is helping to meet.

We all have needs; the most basic needs include to be LOVED, to be WANTED, to be APPRECIATED. There are others of course, and each of us goes about fulfilling these needs our own particular way. When you can question your belief in the above manner, you may find that some alteration to your belief may allow some of your resultant thoughts / behaviors to alter and by doing so, alleviate your emotional pain / suffering / anger.

NOTE. Your NEEDS are not to be confused with your WANTS.

CHAPTER 1

EXPECT AND RESPECT DIFFERENCES

After a lengthy discussion with Dr. M. ALAM from Dandenong Mental Health Service, he imparted the above wisdom to me. This phrase means quite a great deal when applied to our psychology.

Each one of us has to EXPECT other people to have different beliefs, behaviors, rules, values, standards, morals, and ethics, etc. as we are fortunately not "cloned" copies of each other, we are unique. We will never find another human being with exactly the same beliefs, etc. Just as well, it would be a bit boring if we were all the same.

Knowing and accepting this fundamental truth, will lead us to the next truth. We must RESPECT these differences we encounter if we want peace and harmony in our lives, and our world. We must live by the rule of "live and let live." We cannot force our beliefs onto anybody, or any race, or, any country.

If this sounds unrealistic to expect and respect each individual's right to their beliefs, then examine your own beliefs to see whether they are based on laws of the universe, or just your interpretations of these laws. Be careful of the meanings we invent for our mind to digest and turn our lives into a tangled web of complicated rules and regulations. Not everyone knows your rules and regulations, besides they are just your rules, your mode of operating in your world, as you see it.

How much pain and suffering do we create for ourselves when we expect others to abide by our rules? It would be unreasonable to expect everyone to conform to your rules, now, wouldn't it?

It is everyone's' right to have differences, whatever they may be. Obviously some will be minor, some major, some tolerable, and some intolerable. We allow ourselves to be "suspect" I believe, when we force others to accept our differences. That is to say, "this is how it is, no question!"

Grasping the concept of expecting differences, and respecting differences for what they are, allows one to find acceptance of each other easier. Naturally when there are fewer differences, especially major differences, then our "matching" up process, that seemingly impossible quest to find your "soul mate" is simplified.

Having a huge number of "major differences" to contend with, may mean quite a bit of help is needed to unravel the fundamental core reason for maintaining these beliefs, which may be based on false perceptions, and not reality or truth.

RECIPROCAL COMPREHENSION

What a mouthful. I heard this phrase talking with an 85year old dear family friend. She was explaining some of her observations of her life to me.

Basically it relates to the ability of people to understand each other.

When two or more people communicate, what they comprehend is not based only on the spoken word. Science has shown that non-verbal communication is responsible for giving us signals, which we interpret together with the verbal words spoken.

These non-verbal signals, quite often give each one of us different messages to the words being spoken. Have you ever played "Chinese whispers?" What each person interprets is exactly that, our individual interpretation. What this "reciprocal comprehension" means is each person in a relationship, whether social, business, or intimate, needs to reach this level of mutual understanding. Where every person involved is able to interpret the true meaning of what is communicated, they are on the same "page", as it were.

How often do we come across instances in our life, where miss-understandings occur?

We all react differently to life. Based on the basic four causes (refer chapter 2). Add to these, our body language, adding it's' slant to what is being communicated, is it any wonder the world is being torn apart, not only by broken relationships, but also through communication breakdown, and this happens at all levels, including governmental.

Reciprocal comprehension is absolutely mandatory for clear and precise communication between two or more people. Without it we create division, misunderstandings, conflict and pain.

This book, I pray will assist you to understand how this process occurs. I have the utmost faith that it will benefit you all.

HOW DO WE ACHIEVE ACCEPTANCE?

The principal of acceptance is a fundamental one we need to establish in our life.

Every human being has their own view of their world, as they know it. That is the world they have created within their own mind, based on their beliefs, values, environment, and the overall cause.

What I mean by "overall cause", is simply this; we are part of a whole, and as such, have limited capacity to influence the entire collective. Consider this; our bodies are made up of approximately 50 trillion individual cells, how stupid would it be if only one cell controlled all the others.

Similarly, as we live on planet Earth, with over 7 billion other human beings and countless billions of other creatures, how can only one influence the entire whole?

As everything that exists is energy, and is interacting with energies that are entangled in a quantum soup that is universally present, and, this field, as Einstein stated, is all there is, how can one possibly separate themselves, from this field.

The overall cause is weighted against the individual . . . . until critical mass is reached.

I am sure most of you are aware of this term, and for those that are unfamiliar with it, a short explanation follows.

There comes a point in life, any life, even that of cells, where change occurs when sufficient numbers combine to cause a different outcome.

This is evident in our own bodies when related to any disease. It is only when sufficient cells within our bodies combine together and send the same signals, that we are able to feel pain, or for that matter, pleasure.

Our individual interpretation of the way we look at events will be influenced entirely by our unique experiences of life as we sense it so far.

This is the key to acceptance. We all have individual, unique lives. Each of us has our own "world", so to speak, in which we live. This is the internal world within each of our individual minds. This is similar to the theory "men are from Mars, women from Venus", only more so, due to the total number of human beings on planet Earth. Knowing that we will all view the same thing differently means we have to develop a sense of TOLERANCE. Just because someone has a differing belief that is not in line with yours, doesn't mean you are right, they are wrong.

When you put this right or wrong spanner in the works, you make life too complicated for all. Simply by allowing your focus to find some alternative meanings can alter your view of the situation. Using the common "problem solving" technique, where both parties in disagreement, put forward their suggestions to resolve the matter. Each party then examines all the various solutions, and decides which ones are acceptable to all parties. These then get implemented, and if unsuccessful, the process is repeated, until a win for all has been reached.

Practice makes perfect, and this is sometimes difficult. However a tolerant attitude toward each other, especially with the ones closest to you, will make for a happier life, not only for you, but also for them. Remember the K I S principle. Keep It Simple.

The more rules we have in our life, the more we are going to get hurt by others. Not everyone we come in contact with will know our rules. Besides these are just your rules. You invented them. You made them a must, or must never. You choose to complicate your life with these rules. Lighten up a little. Allow your life to experience the joy of freedom. The fewer rules, the fewer stumbling blocks, the smoother the journey.

When you have so many standards / rules, you expose yourself to a multitude of areas where your peace of mind is disturbed. Your inner sanctum is where you can be one with the universe, anything that robs you of this inner peace, robs you of your enjoyment / quality of life.

The mind / body / soul, is a finely tuned mechanism which we have yet to fathom completely. I believe that the disturbance of our inner peace, your mental state of tranquility, is a major factor in contributing to symptoms in our body which show up as various forms of aches, pains, ailments, from the common cold, to other "disease" such as blood pressure, diabetes, obesity, and even cancer, among others.

When you feel upset, disturbed, angry, you are sending negative emotions through your body. These negative feelings cause you to feel down for a period of time. Your state of inner balance has been disturbed, and you need to make adjustments until balance is restored.

This state of disturbance can be avoided by not having so many rules to live your life by. The more rules, the less likely you are to be content with your life. If you have a multitude of rules that have to be satisfied before you feel happy, the chances are less likely that you will be content all the time. Happier are those who have the least amount of rules possible.

Another point to make with regard to rules is that you must realize that these rules / standards are yours. Those close to you do not necessarily share them. If you expect everyone you are close with to have the same standards / rules, then you are setting yourself up for an almost impossible task. We all have learnt different ways of achieving pleasure in our lives. What makes each of us happy or sad may not be identical.

We can all have as many rules / standards for our own life as we see fit. The trick is not to insist on others you are close with to have the exact same rules / standards. Utopia only exists in heaven. We need to develop a sense of tolerance toward each other. Accept that your rules are just that, your rules. They may or may not be identical with others in your life, not even your partner / significant other.

Develop a sense of a free spirit. Allow others this same free spirit. You will be amazed at the resulting effects in all avenues of your life. The trust that develops when you allow the other person to experience this freedom will give you a sense of rock solid foundation. Your total faith in the person will take away any fear you have of losing them. And if their spirit moves them out of your life, then this was not your soul mate. Move on freely and enjoy the journey.

There are areas in life you cannot control, Mother Nature, other people, anything that you do not initiate, you have no control over. The only thing you have complete control over is what things mean to you.

CHAPTER 2

WHO ARE YOU? WHERE ARE YOU? WHAT DO YOU WANT TO BE WHEN YOU GROW UP?

I'm sure you have all heard these questions before, and then some. Let's look at the last question first.

What do you want to be when you grow up? The "WANT TO" part is relatively simple. This includes such things as dreams, goals, aims, aspirations and the like. The "WHEN YOU GROW UP" part is a little more complicated. "When" is obviously the time, the "GROW UP" part, refers to not only the physical body in terms of age and muscle strength, but also in terms of maturity of mind and spirit, and strength of character. It is this area I would ask you to consider the following.

Let us base our discussion by the acceptance of a law of the universe:-

CAUSE & EFFECT.

If you doubt this law exists, please refer to Isaac Newton, Albert Einstein, and another famous person who reportedly stated almost 2000 years ago, "AS YOU SOW, SO YOU SHALL REAP". We have many modern derivatives of this, such as "give and take", "what you put in, you get out", "what goes around, comes around", and in computer terms, "garbage in, garbage out". I am sure you know many more similar phrases.

Understand and accept that WHERE you are at this point in life is a sum total of all the effects that the various cause have had on your life. These causes are summarized here simply as THE NATURE, THE NUTURING, THE ENVIRONMENT & GOD.

Most of these causes are out of our control, or influence. However, we are in complete control of assigning "MEANINGS" to them. The meanings or significance, we attach to the various events (spoken word or action), will determine the thought process we allow ourselves to engage our minds in. If we choose to allow our minds to assign negative meanings, we tend to have sad and negative emotions. That's ok, so long as you don't allow yourself to go into the "snowball effect", which happens when you stack one negative thought on top of another, you know what I mean.

We can stop this process very quickly. One way is to switch your attention or focus, onto some other topic or aspect, of even the event that is causing this negativity. This can be simply achieved by looking at the situation with an inquisitive mind rather than a closed one. Ask yourself this:—WHAT ELSE COULD THIS MEAN? Try and come up with more positive thoughts. Examine alternatives that empower you to look at other scenarios rather than the negative ones you have chosen to concentrate your thinking on, which are based on assumptions you have jumped to. Once you come up with more positive meanings, you automatically get out of your negative emotions and start to feel better about the event.

Know that this is a skill, and like any other, you need to practice at first and keep practicing all your life. We all need to "just do it" as they say, because as we do it, we get better at it. We will never attain perfection at doing it, but we will get more confident in doing it, with the repetition of doing it.

Another important tool is action, or movement. It follows, by the law of cause and effect, that if we want to alter our emotional state, then we can do so by altering our movement.

Examine if you will, the posture of a depressed person, as compared with a joyful happy person. Notice the differences, the facial expressions, the posture, the mood, I could go on but space prohibits. All you need to apply is some sort of action. As simple as this seems, it is often the simple things that work best. Just alter your state a little. This can be achieved in numerous ways, I'm sure you can think of many that do not require any equipment or great expense.

Going for a walk, calling a friend, listening to music, gardening, reading, exercise, whatever you come up with will do, as long as you get up and just do it, instead of allowing your thoughts to wallow in the quagmire of the state you have buried yourself in.

You see, we put ourselves into these states by assuming meanings to events that are not based on reality. However, by our thinking, we convince ourselves that this is reality. This is because our mind cannot tell the difference between images we think of, and events that are actually real. And what we are telling ourselves is not necessarily the TRUTH; it is merely our interpretation of it, as related to our particular life based on our four causes, so far.

We all are in total control, as I have said before, of assigning the meanings to events, I encourage all of you to try and look for empowering meanings in the causes that influence your lives, and I challenge everyone to explore the above passage and if you find it useful, as I have, just do it.

I encourage all of us to GROW into strong mature human beings who help develop others to do the same along the way.

DON'T BE AN EMOTIONAL TIME BOMB /
BE A HUMAN BEING

I would like to explain my philosophy for mental health. In all my dealings with my own trials and tribulations over the course of my life so far, I have learnt many things, some are profound and I pray you also find the following useful.

This knowledge is a basic truth that I try to live by; at times it is harder than others. All I can say is that nearly all of life's experience is based on our unique interpretations of the events unfolding along life's path. The nurturing we receive, the nature we inherit, the environment in which we live, together with GOD'S overall purpose, are all factors that shape us as human beings. Our experiences to date have molded our beliefs, values, standards, and our code of practice. Each one of us will interpret things in their own way, based upon these established beliefs etc. The response to the stimuli, which evokes an emotion, will depend to these beliefs.

All of life's joys and sorrows (feelings/emotions) are brought about by our set pattern of thinking with regard to the experiences we have had. Our brain re-presents the event to us in accord with our established pattern of belief (habit). The trick is to understand whether our belief is based on TRUTH or assumptions we have made. Allow me to explain . . . what we interpret is only that . . . OUR INTERPRETATION based on our beliefs.

It may not be the truth in reality.

Often we assume the worst out of events or even words spoken. We stack negative meanings to them and end up in a tailspin, assuming the person or event has meant it the way we have interpreted it, usually without actually clarifying with the person involved, or analyzing the event, to discover EXACTLY what was meant.

The meanings we place on various stimuli that we are exposed to in our lives determine the quality of our lives.

Imagine if you placed alternative meanings to these stimuli. Instead of assuming the negative or hurtful meaning, you empowered yourself with more positive uplifting meanings. As the following sayings go, EVERY CLOUD HAS A SILVER LINING . . . , ONE DOOR SHUTS, ANOTHER OPENS . . . , and THE BEST IN LIFE IS YET TO COME.

If you were reacting to life, as if on an emotional roller coaster ride, you would do well to try and take CONTROL of your emotions and understand this. All of our emotions are based on our thinking, which is governed by our beliefs.

AS WE BELIEVE SO IT IS DONE TO US. This is not about positive thinking; it is more about the way our brain functions. We attract the things we FOCUS on. ASK AND YOU SHALL RECEIVE. Belief in whatever you want, and concentrating on achieving it, and having faith that you will succeed, will eventually get you the result.

If you are constantly thinking negative or sad thoughts, you will usually be sad and depressed. For example, I can never get it right. How come I seem to attract these partners all the time? I can't do whatever. Etc etc. These questions will only bring more negative emotions and events to your life.

However, if you choose to look at the brighter side, you will tend to be more cheerful and positive. And asking yourself a better question, will usually get a better result.

I am not advocating this to be easy, nor am I saying that we will never experience sad thoughts in our life. What I am saying is that we must accept these feelings for what they are, mere feelings which we can acknowledge and accept from time to time and not dwell on them. We can learn from them and look for the empowering positive alternative meaning they all contain. We can also choose to alter the beliefs we have built up over the years that limit our human experience.

We must understand that we are ultimately in charge of our bodies mind and spirit. If we choose to think better thoughts we will attract a better future. The control is totally in each one of us to examine the meanings we give to the stimuli we are exposed to. We cannot control these stimuli. For the most part they are generated from our environment and the people we are in contact with. However we can totally control the meanings we attach to them. By doing this we can totally control our reaction to life's sometimes sad and harrowing experiences.

CONTROL is the key to preventing us from becoming an emotional reactor. The way to regain control is to understand and re train our minds thinking to the truth of each and every situation. That is, not to assume that this situation is the same as that of the past.

When we are faced with situations that tempt us to react in the negative, stop your train of thinking and ask yourself this question. WHAT ELSE COULD THIS MEAN?

We have to ask ourselves this question so that we can train our thinking to come up with less negative meanings and more empowering ones. This will eventually lead us to being loving and humane towards each other rather than reacting from our past negative experiences.

We must also remember that we are all different and we must respect our individual differences, and when there is an issue that causes disagreement, we need to respect the other person's right to their view based on their beliefs, as they should respect your right to your view. We must separate the issue from the persons involved. Attack the issue NOT the person.

WHAT IS DRIVING YOU?

The answer to this question will be different for each of us, depending on, not only our four basic causes in our life, but also on our individual goals that we set for ourselves.

Do you control your reaction to all of your life's causes? OR Do you allow your reactions to be driven by your "AUTO PILOT", that is, judging the current event, with your established pattern of behavior, based on your belief systems?

The answers to these questions are very alluding, because we don't often stop to take the time to examine our life. We tend to "go with the flow", and we resolve that we can't do anything about it anyway. Besides, our life is "not that bad, it's ok", we can put up with it. The pain we sometimes feel is not that soul destroying, we get over it. Do we though?

The pain I'm discussing here is emotional pain, the one you don't see, but can manifest in so many ways, including physically.

Every moment of our existence, we are exposed to various stimuli (events), which give us signals (messages). These messages are processed by our mind, at a speed that not even I can understand. Nonetheless, our mind, through its' thought process, evaluates these events, and allows us to respond.

Mostly the way we respond is ok, for the event in question. Most of the time we are interacting with others, that also respond in a similar fashion. It is only when we respond in a manner that is extraordinary, that we are seen as over-reacting.

When we over-react to the events unfolding before us, we need to ask, is this appropriate for the current situation? Or, might I suggest, your behavior has been triggered by a minor event, you have been feeling "not that bad about", but finally had enough, and you explode. Just like the last straw that broke the camels' back. You finally reach the point of not putting up with this anymore, not another second, and BANG, aren't the fireworks brilliant.

I'm sure you all can relate to the above experience. Even if you were not the one to explode, you may have been at the receiving end, and wonder what did I do? At the very least, you would know that there are people in our world who behave like this.

This behavior is the result of their fundamental basic causes, their belief systems, their values, their rules, and code of conduct. All of these systems direct their minds thought process. They believe in the reality they have created for themselves. This reality is not based on truth, but rather their perception of the truth. This perception is different for each of us.

We all base our thinking on the truth, don't we?

What is TRUTH?

This is difficult to communicate to everyone, but I will try to do the best I can. The real world I will call all the things we can touch, see, and experience with our senses. The not so visible world, which is also real, is that of the mind, or soul, or spirit.

What our individual mind can focus on, whether real, or imagined, is reality for the individual. Our mind processes thoughts, and formulates our decisions, on real events, as well as imagined ones. We do not have two separate areas in our minds, one for imagined or perceived reality, and another for the true reality. All our thoughts go into one brain.

Our beliefs, that have foundations in imaginations, hallucinations, misrepresentations, or the belief of others, become reality to the individual. But only for the reality of the individual with these beliefs, and the group he shares these beliefs with.

For the most part, we all have some of these beliefs established in our mind, and they serve us well. Or do they?

AS YOU BELIEVE, SO IS IT DONE UNTO YOU.

Sound familiar? What you believe to be true is your reality. If you believe you can't, you will never even make an attempt. If you believe you can, you will, even if at first you fail, you will keep trying and eventually get there. This sounds like positive thinking. But it is more than that. **You attract whatever you focus your attention on. What you resist, will persist.** You can focus on the dark side of life, and many do. This will dig you deeper and deeper into your pit of despair. Your mind does not distinguish between positive and negative. Sure, when you feel pain, your mind lets you know about it, but you are in total control of what you focus on. Do you get the signal, and get yourself out of pain, and learn from your experience? Or do you associate other meanings to the pain, and stay in pain by going back in your memory over all the past events that caused similar pain?

Do you focus on the past, and allow your mind to go into "auto pilot", and respond as always. Or do you respond in the here and now and evaluate calmly, soundly, with detachment, love, and respect for the other person, who has different beliefs?

Once we understand that we can control our thoughts and the meanings we place on the events of our life, even if we cannot control all else, we can at least force our thinking to act with a response based on TRUTH, in spite of our feelings.

It would be unreasonable to expect everyone on earth to have the same beliefs. We need to accept this as fact. When we can, we will be able to improve our life, simply by accepting that our own beliefs may not be based on the reality of others. It follows then, that where there are different beliefs, we need to acknowledge this. And if you cannot accept these beliefs, agree to disagree, without trying to convert each other.

CHAPTER 3

UNDERSTANDING FEELINGS OR NEGATIVE ENERGY / POSITIVE ENERGY

What are they? Where do they come from? What can we do about them?

Is there anything better than the way you feel? I would suggest not.

Every one of us has feelings / emotions, which govern our mood from time to time, every moment of our existence. These feelings we all experience are governed entirely by our own thought processes. We do not get feelings from other people. We might think we do, but the reality is we are in total control of our thoughts and thereby our feelings.

One of the driving forces in our life is the pursuit of pleasure or happiness, and we try to avoid pain, sadness and hurt. We all experience a range of emotions, during our day / life. For ease of discussion, imagine a scale between -100(negative) and +100(positive) I have purposely chosen negative & positive here because there are no good or bad feelings as such, just simply a range of feelings that we all can relate to, and can identify with quickly, and place them into these two categories somewhere along this scale of -100 to +100, depending on the intensity.

Just like a balance sheet, the more positive our feelings are, our life will reflect a more enjoyable and happy one. We seem to cope with all that life dishes out, and when we experience some negative feelings, we have enough resources within ourselves to carry us through. No explanations necessary. At times though, we sometimes allow our thinking to overwhelm us with negative emotions, and we become swamped with negative feelings, leading us deeper and deeper into a state of mind we would rather not be in, but we don't know exactly what to do about it. This is the area I want to explore.

Where do our feelings come from?

What you choose to focus on, you will feel. Our mind perceives reality through thoughts. Thoughts can be based on true reality or imagined reality. The mind interprets our thoughts the same way, wherever they come from.

When we have events occurring in our life, we come up with interpretations of these events. Some experiences are based on reality, and these teach us valuable life lessons. Others are purely based on interpretations or the meanings we attach to the event. The meanings we form are all based on our beliefs. By saying over and over the same self-talk, we tend to create a limiting belief, based purely on our assumptions, or our past.

Our internal language that goes on in our heads, at the sub-conscience level, is based on our life's experiences to date. This language is called "self-talk". At the conscience level we sometimes repeat this talk out loud as well. This is called "verbalizing". The more negative our thoughts, the more negative our feelings. What we feel is determined by what interpretation we choose to put on any event in our life, and not the event itself.

What can we do about them?

Every feeling is sending us a message. They could be positive, or negative. It is the way we handle, or interpret the message that will determine the state of mind we allow our thinking to take us. Therefore it is absolutely critical that we base our interpretation of the events of our life on what is true, what is real, and not on what we imagine, or assume. What is true is dependent on our individual beliefs, values, nature, our nurturing, and environment. In order to gain the truth in every event in our life, we must evaluate the situation soundly. There are some basic questions you need to ask yourself whenever you are faced with an event that is causing you some concern. What is the problem? Is it certain, probable or possible? How important is it? What can I do about it?

Emotion is also linked to the way we move, our motion, or lack of motion. We can alter our emotional state, simply by altering our physical state. We can do very simple things, read a book, listen to music, phone a friend, go for a walk, whatever you want that works. Just do something. Don't wallow in the state you are putting yourself in. You will be amazed at the momentum you develop, when you build up your self-esteem by actually doing something and overcoming the initial fear, which has caused you to have the limiting belief in the first place. Any progress you make will re-enforce you to take further action. You can only build on success, not on failure. If at first you don't succeed, try again, and keep trying until you do.

If something, whatever the goal / aim, seems overwhelming, it is because you have made it too big in your own mind. Break down the task ahead into a set of smaller ones. Set up a map of how to get to where you want to go. Know that every step along the way is getting you closer to your goal. The first step is the hardest, but unless you take that step, you will not even make a start.

Conclusion

It is only by acting with these principles in mind that we can respond to the events in our life with a true and honest action or thought. By re training our thinking, we establish new beliefs based on the truth, and not on our assumptions or miss interpretations. Each event is a new experience, and should be judged accordingly. If we keep pre judging events with our old un-challenged beliefs, we cannot be lead to new pastures. If on the other hand, we choose to let go of our old beliefs, and look at each event with a fresh mind that is open to various views, and not just tunnel vision, we all will reap the rewards.

We need to understand that all of our feelings are simply feelings that we experience from time to time. We do not need to overreact to our negative feelings, but acknowledge them for what they are telling us. When we learn to acknowledge our feelings and not overreact to them, we will automatically take control of our life. We won't be allowing the event to control our life, and thereby sending us the message of hopelessness or despair.

The negativity that we create for ourselves when we assume the worst meaning possible from the events unfolding before us, cause us and those we are close to, immense pain and suffering. Would it not be better to search for alternative meanings, rather than assuming the negative ones? How more pleasant would your life be if you searched for the TRUTH or the REALITY in everything negative that was occurring?

We as mere mortals may never know the truth as to WHY this happened, or they said this, they did this. Sometimes the truth escapes us, and we jump to assumptions. When this involves other people who are struggling with their own issues, is it any wonder there is so much pain and suffering in this world of ours!

CHOOSE YOUR WAY

Choose to adopt the following attitudes in your day-to-day living, and reap the immense rewards that your life will reflect.

Be LOVING.	Be RESPECTFUL.
Be GRATEFUL.	Be CONFIDENT.
Be CO-OPERATIVE.	Be PASSIONET.
Be GENEROUS.	Be ADVENTUROUS.
Be WARM.	Be CURIOUS.
Be PEACEFUL.	Be POSITIVE.
Be KIND.	Be WILLING.
Be CHEERFULL / HAPPY	Be GRACIOUS.
Be OPTIMISTIC.	Have FAITH

All of these attitudes or states of mind will generate a positive energy within you that will radiate out to everyone around you. Remember that what you give comes back tenfold. You have absolute power to choose these emotional states every day of your life.

Imagine if you could achieve these states of mind at any moment in time. Well you can. You need to remember that all your thoughts are controlled by just one person, you. If you choose to entertain the less appealing, more negative thoughts, then you will cultivate those emotions, and they will grow tenfold. However, if you can interrupt your pattern of thinking and implement the above attitudes of mind, your negativity will be overcome.

This is by no means easy, and it takes time to learn, but rest assured this does work. Eventually these newer ways of thinking will multiply and outgrow the attitudes that have remained unchecked for years, and have caused pain and suffering in your life.

LOVING

Be loving toward others and also love yourself. Love is all encompassing, it is difficult to describe in a sentence or two. However when you are full of love for yourself, you can begin to share your love with others. Loving yourself means basically you respect your BODY, MIND, & SPIRIT. Obviously when you share this love with another, you respect their body, mind, and spirit as well, as if it were your own.

Take care of your body, look after it, it's the only one you have. Stop abusing your body. Your health and hygiene are extremely important. Your body is a complex creature with intricate systems working all the time without you even consciously making an effort. Take better care of your body, and it will last you a lifetime.

Your mind and your spirit also need to be respected in relation to your whole self. Allowing your mind to be corrupted with "weeds" will prevent you from achieving your full potential. Be very careful of what you allow your mind to cultivate. I accept that we all get inundated with information; however it is up to each one of us to select / choose the useful stuff from the rest. Our mind is a sponge, absorbing everything. We decide what gets entrenched, what to focus on, what to think about, what to talk about, and what importance to place on the information.

GRATITUDE

Be grateful for all the things in your life that you actually HAVE. This includes all those intangibles such as the love and respect of other people in your life, as well as all those things we all take for granted. Things like our sense of smell, which enables you to appreciate a rose for instance, or our eyesight that allows you to see God's wonderful creation. Just think of all the things in your life that you are grateful for. I am sure your list will be quite long if you sit down and really try hard to recall all of your "possessions", especially when you include all of your material items as well.

Concentrate on your ASSETS and not your LIABILITIES. As soon as you look at what you do NOT have, you will be heading in the opposite direction and allowing your focus to wander into negative territory. This is to be avoided, stay with the assets, or the positive side of the ledger.

THE CHOICES WE MAKE WILL DETERMINE THE STATES WE LIVE IN.

<u>What do I mean by this?</u>

Basically each one of us has the decision to make at every step of your journey through life. You choose between this or that, doing one thing or another, getting an ear stud or a belly stud, or both and then some. Everything you do is a choice you have made. A choice is a decision, a decision you make, influenced of course by your beliefs, values, morals, peer group, etc.

We as capable humans, have the most wonderful tool at our disposal, the power to choose. This power needs to be exercised very wisely indeed, as the choices we make determine our destiny in life. Our mind is constantly making choices / decisions at every level of our consciousness, (I have heard there are about 100 levels). Most of these choices we are unaware of, we are on automatic pilot so to speak. The ones we do know about are those we make at the conscious level.

This power to choose is I believe, a tremendous source of energy that we need to tap into. When you realize that the power to ALTER your choice is also available to you at any time. That is, you can alter your decision, if the outcome was not what you wanted, and make another one. This process can be repeated until you achieve whatever you wish to achieve.

The choice is yours. You, and only you, choose to believe that you can do it, or you can't.

Furthermore, the general state of mind we allow our brain to go into, I believe, can be very much determined by the positive choices we make. The choice to be basically good, rather than evil, the choice to look at the bright side, rather than the dark, the choice to be helpful, rather than obstructive, the choice to be kind, generous, happy, adventurous, etc, are all choices we can make.

These positive states of thinking, will lead you to a much brighter feeling of well-being, and your brain will thank you for not burdening it with the draining, negative, recurring, destructive, de-stabilizing thinking that can occur from time to time.

One final thought, is a piece I read recently.

"The longer I live, the more I realize the impact of ATTITUDE on life. Attitude, to me, is more important than facts. It is more important than the past, than education, than money, than circumstances, than failures, than success, than what other people think or say or do. It is more important than appearance, giftedness or skill. It will make or break a company, a church, or a home. The remarkable thing is we have a choice every day regarding the attitude we embrace for that day. We cannot change our past. We cannot change the fact that certain people act in a certain way. We cannot change the inevitable. The only thing we can do is play on the one string we have, and that is our ATTITUDE.

I am convinced that life is 10% what happens to me and 90% how I react to it."

<u>This means basically, that our reactions to issues, events, situations, what is said, etc, is dependant mostly upon our ATTITUDE. YOUR SILENT PARTNERS</u>

Increase your awareness of them.
Learn how to use them in everything you do.
Understand that they assist you both ways.
Know that it is your choice every time.

Your partners are always with you in good times and in bad times.

CHAPTER 4

WHAT SEEDS ARE YOU SOWING?

How many of us believe that what we plant or sow, will eventually develop into mature fruit of our labor, if we tend to the various requirements of the plant during its' growth?

Those who have green thumbs will attest to this, I am sure. You will also relate to what happens if you neglect the plant, and allow weeds to take over your garden.

When we receive or better still, PERCIEVE, signals or messages, from the events unfolding in our life, do we cultivate harmful, destructive, sad, painful, or other negative thoughts? Allowing them to multiply in our mind, just like weeds in your garden, or do you dig them out, and replace them with better thoughts.

Your mind is the ultimate garden. Whatever you plant in it, will grow and eventuate for you, creating your reality. You will reap whatever you sow, this includes weeds.

May I suggest that if this applies to you, you may want to cultivate the following thoughts instead? If you remove the weeds, you need to replace them with something else, don't you, or they will come back, will they not? Possibly the following could be useful to cultivate in your garden. Thoughts of love and harmony, appreciation and gratitude, excitement and passion, confidence, accommodation of others needs, health and happiness, faith, not only for the future but in God or a higher power if you prefer, determination, flexibility, contribution to others, cheerfulness, smile be happy. These are by no means the only positive thoughts you can think of, I'm sure you may think of many more.

One fact that has been proven time and time again, and that is that the longer you leave the thought in place, just like a weed, it grows. Eventually if left unchecked, they take over. Try not to let this happen. Deal with issues at an early stage; the process will be less painful. It is far easier to deal with tiny seeds, than giant trees. Ultimately all our thoughts, by repetition, grow and develop our character, into maturity.

This maturity is not only viewed in the one dimension, but also through the sense of one's spirit, soul, or heart. Grow your maturity, by cultivating healthy attitudes to life. Cultivate the habit of generating the positive thoughts, consciously. Set up a time for yourself every day, where you can recharge your mind with these thoughts. First thing in the morning is probably best. This way you start your day off on a good note, on a "high" if you like. You will be amazed at the results, you have nothing to lose.

WINDING UP AND WINDING DOWN.

We all experience times when we seem to be wound up that little bit tighter than usual. Most of the time we seem to manage our levels of stress quite well. There are many strategies we can use to cope with tension. Sleep is one of the most beneficial restorative processes we have at our disposal. There are a number of other strategies we can employ, and I will go into these later. For now I will concentrate on the process that takes you from normal everyday stress to being wound up so tight that you actually could snap or break down as many people do.

Similar to a guitar string that is properly tensioned, we need a certain amount of stress or tension to perform. When there is insufficient tension, or too much tension, the string will not sound the same note and will be out of tune. This is purely a crude analogy to make my point. However we humans will also go out of balance if we undergo too much or too little stress.

Taking the case of too much stress, we can see that a person will keep stacking their little irritations that accumulate during the day, week, months, years, to a point where the normal methods of coping do not help any more. Their mind seems to get tangled up with all the problems, issues, and negative aspects of the event or situation. The assumptions they make lead them to believe that whatever the reason their mind has conjured up to be the only certain reason for the event in question. This negative thought process leads them into a deeper and deeper state of anxiety, which eventually can lead to feelings of fear, hopelessness, and overwhelming depression.

When your mind formulates these certainties, we seem to accept them as being the truth. The problem is however that these feelings have been generated not by the truth but rather by the individuals own thought processes.

Certainty is power.

When we have certainty, when we are clear about things, we know where we are going, we know what to do, or at least we can figure it out. This process is going on all day long in our minds. We are continually making decisions and responding to the events unfolding before us. This decision making process usually happens so quickly that we do not even realize our mind is at work. Sometimes when the issue is more important to us than the everyday, run of the mill stuff, we need to think a bit harder about things before reaching a decision. At times, some issues are extremely important to us and we have to struggle with this process for longer periods, the answers are not readily formulated in our mind, they are more complicated than usual. Sometimes it is difficult to carry out a decision even after careful evaluation of the issues.

When a decision is reached and acted upon, you empower yourself with momentum to move forward. Even if you made the wrong choice, you will have learnt this information and you can correct your next action. Try and try again, as the saying goes.

Obviously you need to exercise sufficient care in reaching the decision. Having regard to all the risks involved, it would be foolish to just make wild choices and keep going with this process until possibly you stumbled on the proverbial needle in a haystack.

Misplaced importance

We all have issues that are important in our lives. Some issues are more important than others, while some are absolutely crucial for us that we will do anything to preserve them. Your health is one such issue, if not the most important next to happiness.

I believe some of us lose track of this simple truth. We make our job or our family, or our sport, or our addiction, or money, or some other issue our most important focus in our life. Some of us have a huge number of issues that are all up there at the top of the list with health and happiness, that it is difficult to separate one from the others.

Unfortunately when this occurs, our decision making process becomes clouded. We tend to overlook the issues of health in particular, and place other concerns over and above it. After doing this for a number of years I know only too well what the results can lead to.

Your health and happiness, I believe, go hand in hand as the most important aspects in life. Without your health you cannot enjoy life fully. Without happiness, what enjoyment is there in life? Health is achieved through looking after yourself, physically, mentally, and spiritually. Happiness comes from within one's own thought process. If you are unhappy, it is not up to other people to make you happy, but rather you need to re evaluate what is making you unhappy. Have you misplaced importance on something that is precious to you and not others? Has this misplaced importance clouded your thinking, making you unhappy? Remember you are in total control of the thoughts you allow your mind to cultivate.

What you focus your attention on will eventuate for you. First in your thoughts, and then in your physical world. Think about it. Everything you have today was once only a thought.

CHAPTER 5

HOW CAN WE CHANGE?

The basic changes, for the development of a new self, are through three methods. We can change our thinking and talk, our actions or ways, and our relationships. There are many methods available today for people interested in changing CERTAIN ASPECTS OF themselves. Countless therapies, modalities and re-habilitation methods exist that basically are all effective in self improvement.

All the above methods will work on our own self ALONE. We cannot force others to change, no matter what we might try, excepting force. We will develop new outcomes for our lives, when we initiate an alteration, no matter how small, in any of the above areas. This is based on the law of cause & effect.

One thing to understand, which is extremely important, I believe, is that while each one of us is going through our change, those around us may not be supportive. They may be happy with you as you are, at their level of maturity or understanding. They may not recognize the need for change; they are quite content to "keep on keeping on". Even when things go wrong in their life, they are happy to blame others for their lot, refusing to acknowledge that they have at least contributed. Mostly these people are the ones' closest to you. It is one of the most difficult decisions to make, I have found, to end a relationship with someone you were intimate with.

Often we try and encourage the partner to change as well. This usually meets some resistance. They seem to believe that it is you that needs to change, not them. While this is so, they fail to realize that your change will cause different future outcomes for both of you.

Acceptance of the inevitable outcome, associated to change, must precede any change.

When you are faced with a challenge that involves your partner, you need to try and incorporate their support and their involvement. This will allow you to share your progress, obtain feedback, and continue changing, together.

However, I have found, when your partner does not accept any responsibility in the challenge you face, they will attempt to sabotage your progress and keep you down at their level. This is when you need to determine whether your relationship with this person, or group of people, needs changing.

Often we find the answer to this much later in our relationships, usually after some time together, and possibly after having children with this partner. Life gets' pretty complicated for us at times. Wouldn't it be wonderful, if we all could be given a set of instructions at birth, to guide our decision making process.

I believe that mans' ability to learn, is allowing us to do just that. Man can learn from lessons of life, as well as from those that have gone before. There are many examples to follow. Many "mentors" as they are called today. Any one of us can model ourselves along the lines of successful people. There are books, videos, tapes, cd's, seminars, talks and so on. I believe there is a very famous person we can all follow, his name is JESUS CHRIST.

Having said that, allow me to elaborate on the three basic methods we can use to make change in our lives.

Firstly the simplest method is our movement, or our actions, in the way we engage our muscles. What we do with our physical body will impact on our mental state, our emotions. Remember our body, mind and spirit is all connected to one person, you. What you do in one area affects the others.

As simple as this seems, even minor shifts in our actions can cause major changes in our lives. For example, it would be hard to maintain a sad feeling if you wore a smile on your face.

The next area is our thinking, our self-talk, and our perceptions. This is one of the most complex areas we can have to deal with. We all have our own beliefs and convictions, values, morals, ethics. We are all individuals and will interpret things differently, based on the above beliefs etc. therefore suffice to say that when you find yourself reacting in a negative way to an event, simply remember that there is a reason for everything. That empowering reason may not be evident to you there and then, but nevertheless there is always a reason for everything. Please refer to other chapters for greater explanations.

Finally our relationships can change. This does not mean that you are no longer a son or daughter, father, mother or whatever. It simply means that your relationship with a particular person will change. This change may be expressed in many ways, not necessarily only in termination of it. Please refer to the chapter on relationships.

The KEY element for change is to become more aware of your thoughts, actions, and perceptions, at the moment you are experiencing life, and to control yourself from responding in your usual "automatic" style, and instead, using the knowledge gained via any therapy you have taken, make a better choice. That way you will gain a different outcome, hopefully a better one.

Albert EINSTEIN was quoted as saying that you can never obtain a different result, by doing the same thing over and over.

Whatever you do that is different, will make a difference. Little by little, these differences will grow and eventually, you will have re-trained your auto-pilot to respond more to the truth of the situation rather than your "interpretation".

CHAPTER 6

ULTIMATE POWER TO RECREATE YOUR WORLD NOW

You have the power to create a world for yourself that is all you want it to be. This power is universal, and is available to all human beings. We all can choose to base our decisions, which ultimately control our life, on the truth of reality, rather than basing our decisions on our beliefs or rules, which have been built up over the years. These beliefs may NOT be based on reality. Our response to events in our life, usually are spontaneous, based on our belief systems, our rules, our values, our environment.

Each individual mind can, if it chooses to, look at any and every event in their life, through another perspective. Looking for the "silver lining", or the empowering meaning, must lead you to view events in a light that will allow you to make better decisions. Every event has a purpose. This purpose we need to seek out, sometimes it is harder to find an empowering meaning, but it is there. We have to look harder, and possibly look outside the circle / square.

Are you thinking as if you are the center of the universe? Possibly you need to decentralize from yourself, and step into eternity. Is the way you are reacting, just about you? Or are there other people concerned? Is the event directed at you, or your behavior? Mostly events are not about you personally, but rather, the issue in question. Sometimes we jump to wrong conclusions. Sometimes we misinterpret events and give our brain incorrect information to process. Often the people we have relationships with, are caught up in their own troubles. They also are struggling with their own needs and issues, you simply happen to be there at this point in time. The interaction of two or more minds with differing beliefs / rules, becomes entangled, causing enormous heartache. Is it any wonder there are so many broken relationships in our world today?

Even in death, there is an empowering meaning. At the very least, the person is not suffering any longer. An even better meaning is that their spirit is re-united with their creator, GOD, or the overall cause if you prefer. If you believe in heaven, then you can choose to be glad that their journey of suffering on earth, has concluded, and their journey in the afterlife has begun.

The most significant meanings to the events of our life, are the ones that empower our decision making process. Therefore it is crucial these meanings we formulate for our lives, are based on the truth of reality, and not based on our prejudices, or our past, or worse still, on the beliefs of others.

To achieve the truth, we simply ask ourselves the following question.

What else could this mean?

Keep asking this question until you get at least as many positive alternatives as the old negative ones you automatically jump to.

This alone will force you to take control of your negative thought process, and if you consistently apply this practice whenever you experience a negative feeling, you will empower your mind with positive alternatives, which will not evoke your usual response. You will be in total control, instead of running on "auto pilot" as it were.

The people we associate with can also influence our perspective of the events unfolding in our life. If you live with cripples, you learn to limp. We can choose the peer groups to associate with. If you want to create a better life, associate with those who have a higher standard. This will inspire you to learn from others. Just like a coach, you will pick up ideas to improve your game. And once you do improve, you get a better coach to take you to the next level.

Sometimes the game of life seems so complicated and difficult that you want to give up, or you have this sense of hopelessness and despair. Maybe we have created this hell on earth, by our mistaken beliefs, which we have formed over the years. These beliefs shape our future actions by shaping our decisions. Maybe we can challenge these beliefs, and re train our thinking to respond to the truth of the event, and not our past experience.

Often we run our life with so many rules, that we get hurt all the time when these rules get violated. Quite often the people in our life do not know our rules. Often we need to ask ourselves, are my rules relevant in this situation. Do we need all these rules anyway?

How is it we have so many rules, for a game of life, that often we don't even have a purpose or a goal to aim for? We can't expect everyone we come in contact with during our life, to know our rules. We need to appreciate that these rules, are simply our rules. We created them over the years. We can also re-create them. The choice is ours.

Whose life is it anyway? Are you leading your life by someone else's rules? Have you got too many rules? Obviously each one of us has their standards, and code of conduct. We all need to appreciate every individual's right to his or her own beliefs. We cannot force our beliefs onto another human being. Each one of us however, can examine our beliefs, and question those that are continually causing pain and suffering. If we find that some beliefs need a shift, so we no longer react with pain and suffering, then the way is clear. Presuming of course you don't enjoy pain and suffering.

Faith in your future, in your purpose for living, in the overall cause, GOD if you will, in eternity, will set your mind free. Having faith, when all else fails, restores your minds power to enable you to make the appropriate decisions. I challenge each one of us to develop a strong connection with this overall power, which is controlling the universe.

Are you up to the challenge? Are you capable of re-evaluating your rules? Are you content to stay where you are, in your mind? Do you deserve better? Do you want to expand your beliefs? Everyone reading this paper is able to take up these questions. You will not regret it because your freedom, your sense of mature character will be your reward. The knowledge that you can control the thoughts your mind focuses on, even in times of extreme stress, will urge you to at least try.

CHAPTER 7

RELATIONSHIPS

I would like to focus on an area that causes so much pain and suffering for many of us mere mortals, and that is personal relationships. I believe the purpose of a relationship is to SHARE your life with the one you love the most. This sharing of course includes the not so pleasant experiences that we all have from time to time, as well as the good times. I believe some important ingredients for a relationship to succeed are:-

- Total and complete honesty.
- Total and complete regard for the other person in the relationship.
- Total and complete separation of issues that crop up from the person involved.
- Willingness to maintain the relationship, work on it continually.
- Total and complete understanding of each individual's point of view.

HONESTY.

Unless there is total and complete honesty between two people, there cannot exist a solid foundation upon which to build on. Complete honesty is when full disclosure is made. It is not complete honesty when significant details are omitted. As soon as there is dishonesty, the relationship suffers, and may never recover.

REGARD.

Each person must take into account the other persons reactions in all things that concern the relationship. There will occur times when one party will be tempted to do things that they know the other party would disapprove. Having total and complete regard will stop you from damaging your relationship. We also include feelings and emotions when we refer to total and complete regard for your partner.

SEPARATION.

When issues / problems arise, you must separate the issue from the person. Attack the problem, not the person. When you attack the person, you are attacking your own relationship with this person, and causing damage to it. Agree to disagree if you must, but always discuss the issue / problem, and not the person, usually it is never about the person, but rather their behavior. In order to reach agreement when disputes arise, use the common "problem solving technique", where each person puts forward their solutions, then various solutions are tried and tested until everyone is happy. This needs to occur before anger and resentment set in, never allow your anger to well up inside you to a point of explosion, it is easier to deal with problems / issues when they are at their seedling stage, rather than as a fully grown tree.

MAINTENENCE.

A relationship is alive with emotions, feelings, and a spirit of unity, which needs nurturing all its' life. This is a work in progress. It is never done, unless the relationship is ended.

UNDERSTANDING.

Mutual understanding, when there are no misinterpretations, not only of the spoken word, but also non-verbal communication, when the meaning, and understanding is identical.

SOLID FOUNDATIONS.

When two people start a relationship, having regard for each other, and unconditional love for not only themselves, but also for the relationship they are building together, then their relationship could be likened to the great pyramids of Egypt. Having a solid base, and with every other stone leading to "one" at the very apex or top, which you could call the ultimate love they each share for one another.

Conversely, when two people start a relationship, and have less regard for each other, and their "love" is based on possibly the physical, or the chemistry they generate, or any of a number of other factors, then I believe their relationship is doomed and will fail.

The reason also can be likened to the pyramid. As the couple builds this relationship, over time, they are stacking the smaller stones of repression, resentment, resistance, anger, differences, conflict etc. on the outer edges of their layer below. Eventually there will come a time when this structure will be totally out of balance, similar to an inverted {upside down} pyramid, the base cannot support the buildup of all these negative feelings over the passage of time, and will not be, at the very least, as strong as it otherwise could have been.

Every relationship could be a strong one in my opinion, provided that both parties involved, had the above qualities of honesty, regard, separation, maintenance, and understanding. Sadly, there are many examples today and indeed throughout history, where these qualities were missing.

I wonder sometimes, how could this knowledge, be taught to our future generations so they will hopefully be better informed before they embrace an intimate relationship. Often by the time some people acquire this knowledge, they have already been scared by previous failed relationships. Unfortunately this scaring makes them wary of future relationships, and often leads them to a solitary existence.

How sad they deny themselves the pleasure of sharing their life with someone.

LEVELS OF RELATIONSHIPS.

The best way to explain this concept is to imagine the whole human race as being made up of billions of total strangers. As you progress up through the levels of each individual relationship you form, you could regard yourselves as acquaintances, then move on to becoming friends in the many categories, such as work mates, play friends, social, personal, family, and intimate.

Also within each type of relationship, you can have different levels. For example, let's take an intimate relationship between two people. On occasions, there will be issues / problems that erupt in the relationship. Depending on how they react to the issue / problem, the relationship can move either way. If they are able to keep the issue separate, and have regard for their relationship as well as each other, and maintain all the above qualities for a successful relationship, their relationship will only grow stronger into the next level. On the other hand, if either one personalizes the issue, or possibly looks for someone to blame, or has little understanding of the damage caused to the relationship when they attack their own "ship" and fight, argue and otherwise cause rifts to appear, then that relationship moves downward to a lower level. Sometimes if this pattern is repeated often, the relationship has nowhere else to go and crumbles through separation and divorce, and often causes untold damage to all concerned, including possible children, and the community at large.

Can you see that even within an intimate relationship, there may exist different levels, of intensity at least, from time to time?

Most of us enjoy some sort of an intimate relationship that sea-saws between the highest levels, and those levels where it's not so brilliant for a while at least. For some people this sort of situation is the norm, they accept it as "that's life", and feel powerless to do anything about it.

I believe the answer lies in the ability to keep the relationship completely separate from any problems / issue that inevitably crop up over time. Obviously where the issue is of major proportions, then differences need to be ironed out to mutually agreed solutions, and where this is not possible, one needs to assess the importance of it all. By this I mean the importance of whatever is causing the problem between the two, and where is it in regard to the overall priorities of the couple, or person concerned.

Sometimes parties dispute over trivial, insignificant issues which really are made important in the mind of only one of the people in the relationship. The dispute is related to the persons' beliefs, values, and code of ethics, which have been developed by that persons' nature, environment, nurturing, and the overall cause, God.

Parties in an intimate relationship, I believe, need to let go of issues that are of little consequence. Keep their aim / goal on building a strong, loving relationship, maintain a certain detachment from minor issues, and reserve disputes / conflicts, only for the major issues that crop up. I believe these major issues are not found in everyday, run of the mill, living.

There are plenty of people who put a lot of their energies in the minor issues of everyday life, with resulting high levels of stress, anxiety, and even depression. All this does is place extra burden on the relationship, and at times when major problems come up, the parties have spent most of their energies fending off the minor issues, they have little left to take the correct steps necessary now, when most needed. Relationships suffer as a result. Not to mention the health of the people involved.

UNDERSTANDING THE BONDS

Here I will attempt to explain the bonds that are created between two people who share an intimate relationship. I will also explain why I feel it is important to release your ties with this person, once the relationship is no longer one of intimacy, but merely friends, as so often happens in broken marriages / relationships.

Firstly let's examine the universal symbol of LOVE.

The HEART shape is, I believe a commonly used symbol of love. Two hearts overlapping are often the symbol of lovers. I hope you can all agree so far. Imagine the latter case of two hearts becoming one as it were, which is usually what most of us accept as the concept of unity, marriage, togetherness. Two hearts joined together, sharing their life together.

Each person in this relationship tries to fulfill their partner's wants, and needs, to the best of their ability. Hopefully they are good at expressing their wants and needs to each other and life progresses smoothly for both people. We all know that there are a multitude of wants and needs that exist today, however I will focus on just a few.

Love and warmth, security, tenderness, appreciation, care, attraction, generosity, excitement, passion, respect, compassion, I'm sure there are many I have missed, but imagine your heart has as many compartments or rooms, if you prefer, and each of your wants and needs has its own room.

In a healthy and strong relationship, these wants and needs are mostly met by each person within the relationship. This is not to say that other people around you do not fulfill some of your wants and needs, this would be ludicrous. I am specifically containing my focus on the intimate needs and wants, two people share with each other.

What happens when an intimate relationship ends, for whatever reason, the people involved need to allow their hearts to heal. I believe this healing process involves the releasing of the bond held by the other party in the relationship to those rooms of the heart that were once occupied by this person.

Only after empting your room, (within your heart) and creating a void, can another person attempt to enter this room and fulfill your desires, which were previously met by someone else.

When someone has "baggage", their heart is still full of bonds, invisible they may be, but as strong as iron chains. And it is these bonds that will hinder the person from moving on in their life in order to allow someone else to come in totally.

These bonds are often times not even discussed openly. Not with the former partner, nor the current one. People just seem to "go with the flow".

I believe the key to moving on is very simple. Simple to say, but extremely difficult, to do.

Forgiveness is explained elsewhere in this book, but this is the key to allowing yourself, to move on, and allowing the other person to do the same. Let's not forget that this needs to occur from both sides, quite often we see examples of one party to a failed relationship seemingly moving on, but the other party will maintain the bond that existed between them, and re enter the room that the new partner is trying to get into.

Obviously this situation is not good for all concerned. Life is very complex at times and when relationships have failed I believe time is necessary for the healing to take place.

Unfortunately some of us carry within our hearts a torch that is eternally lit for someone other than our current partner. The other unfortunate thing is these torches can be both positive, and negative, depending on where they are placed between love and hate.

This healing can occur at a much faster pace however, when the concept of true forgiveness is embraced totally. In order to forgive we must forgive from our heat, and while our brain can never forget, we must make the effort to suppress the hurtful memories when they come up. Thereby not re-living the experience over and over.

CHAPTER 8

LOVE

I would like to share with you some qualities relating to LOVE, which I am sure you are aware of already, and some that may be new to you. These are by no means the only qualities that are incorporated in the word love, but sufficient for the purpose of the exercise.

Love is good, not evil.
Love is respect for oneself and others, not disrespect.
Love is gentle and kind, not harsh and abusive.
Love is understanding, not misunderstanding.
Love is knowledge, not misinformation.
Love is tolerance of others, not intolerance.
Love is acceptance of others, not rejection.
Love is forgiving, not condemning.
Love is blind, not searching for blame.
Love is caring, not uncaring.
Love is sharing, not being selfish.
Love is pure, not adulterated.
Love is free flowing, not stored.
Love is unconditional, not conditional.
Love is eternal, not ending.
Love is all around, not only in one place.
Love is intangible, yet within reach of us all.
Love is GOD, GOD is love.

To truly love is to love the way GOD loves. Easter reminds us that God loves us so much that he sacrificed his only son in order that our sins of this life are forgiven, and by following in his footsteps, gain eternal life upon our death.

We humans love in many ways, but can never truly love as God loves. Very few examples exist today of true love, and these also can only go so far. The following may come close, Mary MacKillop, Mother Teresa, and Pardre Pio.

We as "mere mortals" have become conditioned to using the word LOVE with great frequency and abandon. We love our sport, we love our job, we love our car, the new dress, or whatever else you may care to mention. We also use the love word with various people in our lives, BUT then we start to ignore what love is all about, and we do the opposite.

I believe that the qualities of LOVE, expressed above, can draw each one of us closer together as human beings, starting with your partner, family, friends, and extending throughout the community at large. Practice, as always makes perfect, but remember, perfection can never be attained, we are constantly improving on our past performance.

CHAPTER 9

ARE YOU LIVING FOR YESTERDAY, TODAY, OR TOMORROW?

How do you look at your time on this journey called life? Do you live in the present moment in time? Or do you spend your time thinking about the future, or the past?

The only time that is real for anyone of us is the present, here and now. The past is gone forever, never to return. The future has not arrived yet, and it may not.

How many of us worry about the future, and what might happen? By so doing, conjuring up all kinds of fear and pain associated about future events that may or may not happen. These scenarios are mere possibilities, not certainties, because they have not happened yet. All this does is overload the mind with worry, and stress. This is so counterproductive to your enjoyment of your life, it is just ludicrous.

Just as pathetic, is the waste of your energy in going over the past events that have caused you pain and suffering. I agree that at times, we must reflect on the past so as to learn valuable lessons. Also it is very therapeutic to recall the good times of the past. This is especially useful for relaxation, meditation, and positive reinforcement. It is only the negative past that I'm referring to here.

Time is a very valuable resource. In fact it is the only thing that is equal for all mankind. There are 24 hours in every day, whether you are rich or poor, black or white, Anglo Saxon or whatever. How much of this time do you waste by spending it on thinking about the future, or the past? Both of these times are not very relevant to our life in the here and now.

All we have is the present time. We need to plan for the future, let go of the past, and live our life in the now.

When you have reached a decision, just do it, now. Do not keep putting it off. This will defeat the purpose, and only delay any outcome.

Make the most of your time. There are only so many tomorrows. We never know what is in store for us, around the corner. When our number is up, we usually do not have a choice.

I am reminded of a song made famous by the Beatles. The lyrics are something like,

"Try and see things my way, we can work it out, don't waste time fussing and fighting my friend, time is very short. We can work it out, try and see things my way".

At times we need to see things from the other persons' point of view, and allow our minds to explore alternatives. This hopefully will bring us all closer together.

CHAPTER 10

ANGER

Anger is an emotion we all can relate to, is it not?

The way we deal with anger is different for each one of us. Some allow the anger to erupt into conflict, while others try and suppress their anger, only to have it dealt with by various methods such as indulging in drink, food, drugs, or a number of other activities which affords some sort of release, or escape.

I would like to share with you my thoughts on anger and more importantly, its management.

Firstly anger is a normal emotion. We all experience occasions that make us angry. There is nothing to fear about this emotion. We need to understand that our response to this feeling is what needs to be addressed, that is if your response is not appropriate already. Usually anger is a secondary emotion that is triggered by a primary emotion. Often we are unaware of this primary emotion, all we seem to feel is the anger. A good example of this could be the following.

Let's say your son or daughter is late coming home, and you have been worried about them, and have rang around a few people, and have worked yourself up into a state. When your son or daughter finally arrives home, your immediate response is to hug and kiss them and ask if they had a good time, yes? Most likely you would be telling them off, and laying down the rules for the future.

As the above example shows, we allow our genuine feeling of love, and concern for our child's well being to be swamped with anger. When this happens we respond to the anger, and not to the primary emotion.

When we react or over react to anger, in a negative way, then we are not helping the situation.

When faced with a situation that is stirring you up to the point of anger, recognize this, and take control. Take control of yourself. Take control of your emotions. Get in touch with your primary emotion. Take control of your response.

By taking control, we will respond to the situation in an appropriate manner. We will not let our emotions control our actions, and thereby aggravating an already tense issue. By taking control, we also decentralize the issue, that is, we do not make it personal. Remember that nothing usually is about you; it's more about someone's behavior. By taking control, you will be able to separate the issue from the people involved, and this will allow you to deal with the issue at the center of the situation, rather than clouding the issue with personal attacks that serve no constructive purpose what so ever.

CONTROL

Count to 10, 20, or whatever it takes. While counting, breathe deeply, and concentrate on breathing. This will help calm your nerves, and help you clear your head so you can deal with the issue in an appropriate manner.

Ongoing issues are not going to resolve themselves. Recognize that you may need to physically remove yourself from discussions several times before any progress is made.

Negotiate, with a clear and calm attitude. Never personalize issues. Never use harsh words, or violent behavior. No one wins an argument.

Turn the energy you have from your anger, and re direct it toward a constructive not destructive outcome.

Respect the other person's right to their opinion and beliefs.

Only keep your angry outburst for the very, very few things in life that warrant it. Most times our every day existence doesn't present us with major issues, such as life or death.

Let your anger be a signal to you that you need to calmly, and coolly, deal with this issue some other time, rather than in the heat of the moment.

IF AT FIRST YOU DON'T SUCCEED, TRY AND TRY AGAIN

This is a very old saying I am sure you have heard it before. However it is worth exploring here. We all have times when we fail at something. It may be in our personal life or in our professional life or in our social areas. The key to learn is that there are no failures in life. There are only learning experiences.

By failing at an attempt, you gain experience at what did NOT work. Learn from this, and try again. If another attempt also fails, you learn that this approach also needs refining. This process continues until you achieve the result you are going for.

You never give up. Once you give up, you have defeated yourself. Your spirit becomes deflated, and you convince yourself that you CAN'T do whatever.

This defeatist attitude creates major hurdles in your mind. Hurdles, that, you alone have put there, simply by giving up.

On the other hand, if you develop and adopt the attitude of persistence, and have faith in your own abilities that you share with all of mankind, you will overcome any failure in your life.

Remember that with faith, and through GOD all things are possible. But you have to do your part. You have to believe there is a way, even when is seems impossible. There are countless stories of individuals who have conquered seemingly insurmountable odds in all walks of life. WHERE THERE IS A WILL, THERE IS A WAY. Belief needs to precede the result. That is to say one needs to believe first, and have faith they will achieve, and then the result will eventuate.

Your determination to overcome the hurdles before you, one by one, will develop solutions for you. You may not be aware of what the solution is, it may just fall into place one day, just trust in the goodness that is provided throughout the universe.

Use all the resources available to you when you are searching for solutions, including prayer. This puts you in direct communication with the most powerful force in the universe. And as you ask, you will receive.

Another powerful resource is to visualize. Imagine whatever it is you are struggling with, as being just right, or working out. See in your mind's eye, the end result, sense the pleasure of finally overcoming this obstacle. Do this often enough and you will be spurred to more and more action in solving your problem.

One final thought, and that is this. Whenever we are faced with problems that seem impossible, you need to employ the above strategies in there correct sequence. You first need to visualize, then ask for help, and then allow for results to eventuate. Some of us expect the results to come immediately. This is not how it works, at least not in most things.

CHAPTER 11

ALL PROBLEMS ARE OPPORTUNITIES

Every time you have an obstacle / problem in your path, do you not try and overcome it?

When you do overcome it, you learn how to deal with this problem, and possibly others that may be similar. This is why problems are always an opportunity to learn.

The way we learn can be very different for each of us, but learn we must in order to expand our knowledge, and progress through our life, maturing like a good cheese or wine.

When you face your problem with an open mind, that is, one that is prepared to accept that all things are possible, then solutions will be found. These solutions may not formulate immediately for you, they may take quite some time to think about and refine. Some you may never find the solution for, on your own, you may enlist the help of others. Using the problem solving methods that are well known, and today are used in dispute resolution, and mediation, as well as in almost every walk of life, people everywhere are exposed to better problem solving methods today than ever before.

Not all of us however are prepared to face some of our problem/s. instead we are happy to ignore it by not dealing with it. Possibly you did try to face it some time back, and it was painful and you gave up your attempts to finding a solution. It was easier to raise that little white flag and retreat within your comfort zone and create this barrier in your mind that limits your growth.

When you have various areas within your life that you have flagged as "CAN'T DO", that is, you have created this defeatist attitude within your own mind, it is my belief you entrap yourself within a cage as it were, and you limit your full potential as a human being. Just like a trained elephant, tied to a stake in the ground with a rope. This poor elephant knows that it is useless to try and get away because as a baby, the rope was a chain, and the stake was a tree, and tug as it might, could never break free. Now that it is older, it remembers the chain, associates the rope as being the chain, and the stake as being the tree, and doesn't even try to get free.

We as GOD'S children are all free to experience the beauty and marvel at the wonders of creation. We have the power within us to choose whatever belief we want to. We can challenge the distorted beliefs / attitudes, and replace them if we choose to. The task is really whether you are up to looking at yourself, at all your limiting beliefs, and taking them on one by one and altering them. Always remember that what you alter will produce different outcomes. (Refer to Cause and effect)

CONFLICT RESOLUTION

How do you handle conflicts or differences of opinions in your life?

Given that we are all unique individuals and we will have different values, perceptions, standards and natures not to mention cultures, we will always experience differences when dealing with others.

Sometimes we will choose to ignore these differences, hoping they will go away. Sometimes these differences are minor and don't pose any real threats. Some are seemingly huge issues that seem so important that we try and convince everyone else that they are wrong and we are correct, that they need to see things your way, and you are so convinced you are correct you are prepared to go to war, so to speak, you dig in and are not prepared to surrender.

I believe the way forward when faced with differences is to first and foremost RESPECT the other persons' opinion. Once you respect their opinion it is easier to come to the table in an atmosphere of peace with a view to searching for a solution. Next comes UNDERSTANDING, which requires hearing the other person. They also have to hear you, and this process continues so that everyone gains greater understanding of the issue and this then leads to SOLUTIONS that are agreed to by all. This may require compromise by both parties and this makes for a WIN / WIN result.

By having respect, understanding and a willingness to compromise, differences can be overcome for the benefit of all concerned.

All this is LOST however when people with differences become confrontational, their immediate response is INFLAMATORY. Almost always differences cause us to become judge and jury, we over generalize, we have that automatic response, I'm right, they are wrong. Without detailing the process, I'm sure you all have had this experience. Just allow me to say that this never leads to solutions, well not the best solution.

Anger is not conducive to the process of bridging the differences between people.

By taking control of your automatic responses, by "biting your tongue", thinking before you open your mouth, looking at things from different angles, try being flexible in your view and not stuck in concrete, look for solutions that will suit all creating the win / win, maintain a cool, calm, and peaceful attitude, solutions will be found.

(Please refer also to the chapter headed ANGER.)

CHAPTER 12

HOW OUR EMOTIONS AFFECT OUR HEALTH

All our emotions have an effect on our physical body.

This is best demonstrated by two very opposite emotions, namely the feeling of "fight or flight" with the accompanying release of adrenalin and cortisol, compared with the joyous laughter which releases endorphins. We can all recognize these hormones and the effect they have on our body. What you may not know is that all emotions transmit signals to our brain. The brain in turn, releases the appropriate hormone in response to the emotion.

The positive hormones I will not mention as they are what we all want, and are beneficial to our health. The ones I am concerned with here are those emotions that cause the release of hormones that lead to an increase in the bloods' acid PH level.

The negative emotions cause the brain to release hormones that ultimately cause the PH level of the blood to become more acidic. In a healthy body, when the PH level rises, your reserves of alkalinity deal with the increase, and flush the excess acid out. However, when these alkaline reserves are used up, the body stores the acid. This acid increase usually manifests itself in your body at your weakest point. This toxic build up can develop various symptoms from minor irritations, flu, aches and pains, including headache and migraine. If left unchecked, these toxin deposits can develop into more serious ailments, such as cancer.

Our emotional state is a major factor in determining the health of our physical body. In today's modern life style, most of us lead very stressful lives. Add to this our intake of foods that are also full of additives, artificial ingredients, and processed to the point that they do not supply the necessary nutrients to our body. Our bodies' natural ability to cope with the acids produced is being severely challenged. Is it any wonder that so many people today, have physical problems, including obesity, addictions, as well as depression, anxiety, and other disorders too numerous to mention?

The remedy is to look at your emotions as a major contributing factor in your physical well-being. Reduce your stress levels. Understand that what you feel at any point in time is directly affecting your health. Try and get into a more positive emotional state as soon as you can after experiencing a negative emotion. Try and not dwell over the negative feeling. Try and look at whatever is causing your negative feeling, and ask yourself "what else could this mean?" Take better care of your body; give it the foods and fluids that aid in the production of alkaline. If you have plenty of alkaline reserves, your body will be healthy. Also try as best you can to incorporate forgiveness in your life.

CHAPTER 13

FORGIVENESS

All of us will say we forgive, from time to time, but then we bring up the issue time and time again. All this does is allow you to re-live the experience, at least within your mind. With the resulting production of the same emotions, feelings as the original first time that event occurred, and your body receives the same signals over and over again. This may cause de-sensitizing over time, but it also causes the buildup of acid in your blood, every time you repeat the story.

I believe the remedy lies in the phrase: "forgive them, for they know not what they do". This forgiveness, I believe, is a must if we are to cultivate a healthy attitude toward others. The spirit of forgiveness also incorporates that of forgetting.

Often you hear people say, I forgive, but I will never forget. The problem with this attitude is that as you re-call the issue, your brain releases the same hormones as those released the first time. Remember, your brain cannot tell the difference between what is real, and what is imagined. This will cause you to re-live the feelings of the past, instead of leaving the past where it belongs, dead and buried.

When you truly forgive and forget, this allows you to get on with life. It also releases you from the pain and suffering that you remind yourself of. Remember this, while you are in the state of mind that forgives, but doesn't forget, you are actually inflicting untold damage to yourself. Whoever you have this resentment for, is oblivious to your pain and suffering. Furthermore, they are probably thinking that everything is back to normal, however, you, and you alone, with this attitude, will continue to punish yourself until you realize that you have to forget as well as forgive. We can never truly forget, however we can choose not to re-live the experience. We can make a conscious decision to stop ourselves from talking about the past hurtful event. When we find our thoughts directed toward the past sad events, be aware that focusing your attention on this painful experience, will only inflict more pain to you. You are in effect rubbing salt into your wound.

You would be far better off to train your mind to focus on the here and now, and let the past serve you as a lesson. Move on with life, and learn to forgive and forget, and if the hurt was too great for you to forgive, may I suggest you ask God to forgive the other party. Once you do forgive, the burden you are carrying will be lifted, and you will free yourself of the shackles holding you to the other person, preventing you achieving your full potential. This could be in any field of human endeavor, but mainly in intimate relationships.

True forgiveness is a skill that too few have acquired. However we as individuals must practice this skill, especially toward the people within our lives. Imagine if we could all practice this attitude with just one person, your intimate partner.

CHAPTER 14

A SIMPLIFIED VERSION OF THE SPIRIT WORLD

Now we are not talking about Jack Daniel, or Johnny Walker, or those spooky ghosts, we are talking about the spirit of love, faith, hope, charity, adventure, courage, wonder, as well as all the other spirits you can think of.

Just about all of our emotions, both positive ones, those that we strive to have most of the time, and the negative, can also be called "spirits".

When someone is said to be in high spirits, we all can relate to someone who is on cloud nine. Nothing seems to bother them, they are riding high, full of uplifting emotional energy. This state of high spirits, is also likened to the animal kingdom. Horses are said to be high spirited when they are bursting out of their skin, eager to be unleashed onto the race track.

This spirit world is the one universal force or energy that is available to each and every one of us. We can tap into it, at our discretion. We can also ignore it, or, not utilize all of the more positive spirits. By the same token, we can choose to tap into the less up lifting spirits. These would include the spirit of hatred, the spirit of despair, the spirit of loss, the spirit of fear, the spirit of depression, the spirit of anger, amongst many others. Simply name a positive feeling / emotion, and the opposite also exists.

I believe that God has allowed all of us the freedom to choose which spirits we want in our lives. This is because we have ultimate control over our thoughts, which govern our feelings.

As explained earlier, we create our responses to everyday events, by the association of what things mean to us. Our interpretations of the events cause us to react the way we do.

So once again, in order to maintain high spirits, we need to seek true meanings to events that unfold before us. We need to look for the positive aspect in even what we initially regard as a low, sad, hurtful, or otherwise negative event.

The spirit world is alive and well. It exists inside each one of us. Most of us pay no regard to the enormous potential that exists within. We busy ourselves with what we can see and touch. If only we knew that the invisible world that is available to all, through the grace of God, is more precious than anything you can materialize.

Imagine the benefits to you when your spirit is aligned with every part of your body and mind.

Imagine the immense power we have once we align our spirit with those close to us.

Imagine this alignment on a global scale.

IMAGINE . . . . a beautiful song by JOHN LENNON.

Imagine a world at peace.

CHAPTER 15

DISTORTED THOUGHT

David BURNS, in his book "Feeling good, the new mood therapy", identifies 10 patterns of distorted thinking. These are:-

1. All or nothing thinking. Seeing things in black or white.
2. Over generalization.
3. Mental filter. Picking up on a negative detail and dwelling on it, darkening your view of reality.
4. Disqualifying the positive. Rejecting positive experiences— "they don't count".
5. Jumping to conclusions. You assume. You mind read. You foretell doom and gloom.
6. Magnification on Minimization.
7. Emotional reasoning. You assume that your negative emotions are reflecting reality.
8. Should statements together with must and ought. Anger, frustration and resentment result in the use of these.
9. Labeling and mislabeling. Attaching negative labels to yourself and / or others.
10. Personalization. You see yourself or somebody else as the cause of some negative event.

We all experience thoughts at times that are not based upon the truth, but rather on our own perceptions which are distorted by any of the above.

Our thought processes are, I believe, entirely generated by our own individual slant we put on events unfolding before us. When we make a situation absolutely certain, we create within ourselves a belief, a truth, that this is what is meant by the event. This belief is what directs our thought process.

Distortions of our thoughts are then causing further complications. This can be seen quite clearly in the case of DEPRESSION. Often the sufferer will be overcome with the hopelessness of the situation. They believe there is no way out, there is no future, that it is useless to even try anymore. (These are by no means the only beliefs, but they will illustrate the point)

The sufferer will then allow their thoughts to become more and more intense by drawing more and more negative emotions from other events that confirm this distorted belief.

It becomes somewhat of a self-fulfilling prophecy.

Thoughts are going on in our minds virtually non-stop. Our thinking is purely our minds way of asking questions, based on all our "filters"(of which beliefs is one), come up with answers. <u>Our ability to direct our thoughts seems to escape us, however we can focus or concentrate our attention, and **we can direct our thoughts**</u>.

By asking better questions, we may get better results.

<u>CLEAR / CRITICAL / RATIONAL THINKING</u>

The skill of practicing clear thinking seems to have been lost in today's world. As explained above, you can recognize various ways by which our thoughts can become "DISTORTED". Our thoughts become clouded and thereby warping our view of reality / truth. (Refer to www. Moodgym.com.au developed by Australian National University)

As these distorted patterns are repeated over time, some can lead you to develop mental attitudes which ultimately cause anxiety, depression, and in severe cases paranoia and psychosis.

WHAT IS THE SOLUTION?

I believe this lies in EDUCATION.

Education starts with the parents, and continues throughout life. Our teachers MUST be trained in practicing CLEAR THINKING. While not telling the student WHAT to think, the teacher must show the student HOW to think clearly, HOW to analyze things, HOW to debate an argument, HOW to evaluate soundly, HOW to spot "distortions" of the truth, HOW to express ideas clearly, HOW to communicate effectively, HOW to "problem solve".

This is surely one way of stemming the predicted increase by the WORLD HEALTH ORGANISATION (W.H.O.) that by 2020, depression will affect 1 in 2 of our population.

We have the knowledge, contained in various books written for psychologists / psychiatrists. We have the education systems, and the subjects, namely English expression. This was a compulsory subject in my days at school.

All that needs to occur is for teachers to be trained in spotting distortions in students work, both written and oral, and explaining these distortions, pointing out where they lie, and showing the student HOW to negate these distortions.

I believe the benefits to society would flow on through many avenues. If people could practice clearer thinking, more rational debate, more effective communication, greater problem solving skills, then, possibly, there could be less expressions of anger and hostility, less divorce, less anxiety, less depression, and who knows what else, the benefits are well worth the effort.

A MODEL EXPLAINING
DISTORTED / WARPED THINKING

We all posses a brain, which can be likened to a computer.

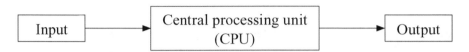

What goes into our brain, gets processed, sorted, and filed away. Some things get absorbed, and some are discarded. Then an action is performed.

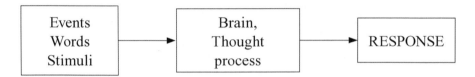

The brain is "programmed" to perform certain manipulations with the information it is given. It does not care what it is given. It simply carries out its' instructions.

When the processing is complete, the decisions are made and action is taken.

However the brain does not distinguish between what the TRUTH is or rather what is correct or not. It simply works with the program that has been installed.

Often times this program is somewhat corrupted.

This unfortunately leads to distortions of the TRUTH, and therefore leads to outcomes that cause chaos and confusion, not only for you, but for everyone else.

Garbage in, garbage out.

Now imagine what happens to a computer when it is corrupted with various viruses.

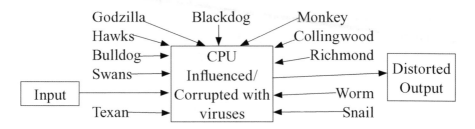

When you have viruses that can influence your capacity to process the input in a true or exact manner, you have distortions of the output.

Just as your computer, once infected with one or more viruses, cannot perform correctly, we humans allow our brains to get infected with various viruses which distort our view of reality.

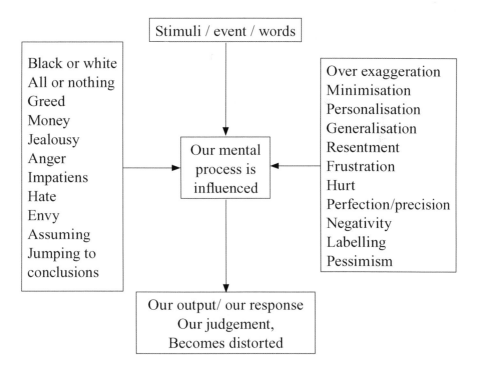

Most computers have "ANTI VIRUS" programs installed to guard against corruption. We humans have no protection whatsoever, save for our own common sense and clear thinking abilities. The problem is however, how can you think clearly if your brain is already corrupted?

The skill of thinking clearly, of using common sense, has been in my opinion, slowly lost over many generations. Everyone's thinking has been influenced to a certain extent, by their environment. When you investigate just this aspect, you can see the impact of advertising, as an example, upon our decision making process. The gentle art of persuasion by reasoning and debate has been taken over by repetitive and sometimes senseless advertising campaigns designed to influence you.

Add to this our own prejudices, our own views, our own natures, and you should be able to relate to how we have all some form of distortions taking place in our thinking process

It is my firm belief that this trend will continue unless an extensive education campaign is put into place.

This education needs to address all aspects relating to HOW to think clearly, as well as HOW to use common sense. The earlier the student is instructed, the easier it is for the student to engage their clear thinking ability, and reason things out with common sense.

Imagine the impact this would have upon society. If we all could exercise extra clear thinking, and extra common sense in our everyday lives.

PERFECT INNOCENCE

Have you ever wondered why newborn babies are so innocent, adorable, cute, and radiate the feeling of love?

The simple fact is that newborn infants have not been influenced by the external world. All they have experienced, in the majority of cases, has been their mothers' womb. This too, has an influence on the baby during gestation. Many studies have shown that the growing baby is directly affected by the mothers' emotions as well as her physical well being.

The innocence of a newborn is possibly the closest being to pure love and GOD that exists. It seems quite weird that life begins with innocence and then progressively as we age, we become corrupted with "un-truths" and as we reach the age of reasoning or maturity, some of us begin to question these lies that we have held for so long, and begin the journey of self discovery.

Have you ever asked yourself the question "what is life all about anyway?"

When one arrives at this stage in their life, important issues surface. Therein is discovered the common denominator that links all life.

This Global, Omnipresent, Denominator.

GOD.

May you recognize the truth, that God IS within you, as God is indeed within everyone.

NAMASTE.

I recognize the spirit within you and respect your spirit.

I come in peace. My peace is with you.

God is with you.

God will do for you, whatever you ask, good or evil.

Gods' will be done.

And so it is.

Amen.

PERSONAL TESTIMONY

My story begins with a tragic event that was to have a major impact on my very existence. When I was 16 years old, and behaving like any other teenager at the time, my parents could not comprehend the rebellious nature within me. They thought there was something wrong, so they took me to doctor after doctor, only to be told that there was no physical problems. They were only trying to avoid loud and aggressive behavior, which was a vexation to my spirit. (Refer Desiderata).

What next? Someone suggested a different approach, so off I went to see some shrink whom I "politely" told where to go. This aggressive behavior was absolutely the wrong reaction. So off I went to an institution. There I was basically locked up overnight, much to my disgust. Shortly after this episode, I suffered another tragedy, the loss of my right eye during a hunting trip. All this happened in 1968, just before sitting year 12 exams (matriculation) for you oldies. I was an angry young man, who had my life turned around by events I had no control of. I soon learned to take complete control, well almost.

At this stage, I felt that my world had completely collapsed. I started to examine my life, asking myself why is this happening. If you want sleepless nights, I recommend this practice to everyone. You will hopefully come to the same answer I found, and that was that ultimately we are not acting alone, in other words, there is a GOD, or at least a higher form of power / intelligence / spirit, call it what you like, which is the overall cause of everything. Then I wondered, what future was in store for a one eyed, aggressive, unstable, Collingwood supporter, who was not in control of his own life?

My emotional state, from time to time, caused me to overreact to various events, in a way that disturbed everyone around me. Usually after these events, I would act or behave in a manner that was "out of character", I was so determined, hardheaded, defiant, whatever you want to call stubbornness, that I was eventually escorted into institutions in order for me to come down to earth, or reality. You see I would work myself up into such a state that I even believed I was the almighty, and I controlled not only myself, but also the entire universe. Not bad for a young kid of migrant parents, who had limited education.

The unfortunate part was that I had to hit bedrock before realizing what you already have, and that is, you have found within yourself the need to improve your life, and are reaching out for help, I didn't reach out, it was forced upon me. I did find some solace however when I saw other people in various worse states than myself. I used to pick myself up from groveling in this endless quagmire. The blow to my self-confidence was, nonetheless, huge. The track record had been established, so every time I behaved out of the ordinary, everyone believed I was going over the edge, and sometimes, I admit, I actually was. I have gained sufficient insight to believe that I am not controlling the entire universe. Just my own little world, which I have built up in my own sub-conscience mind, over my entire time spent alive on planet earth.

What could I do? Would I be successful? What lay ahead?

These and many more questions led me on a pathway of self-discovery. I started to learn from not only life's experience, but also through motivational tapes, short courses, self-help books, whatever I could find. These were mainly stumbled upon through my working environment at the time. Others I sought out, through various counseling I attended during my life. This process is continuing today. As in your own life, we are continually learning and gaining knowledge. I do not profess to know it all, I am the first to admit my own limitations, but I am willing to alter my thinking if shown a better way. This open mindedness, allows you to take on board the challenge of change. Without this open mind, we stagnate in our thinking and our life reflects the rut we build for ourselves, called existence. We do not know, what we do not know. Ignorance is bliss.

Knowledge in itself is great, but it is absolutely useless, unless we act on it. If you know what to do and do nothing, you are a well-educated idiot. Knowing what to do is fantastic, but it won't happen unless you make it happen. You have to do it, and sometimes you just have to trust your newfound knowledge. Practice doing the things you fear, and eventually you will, through constant improvement, gain a different outcome. Remember, everything we do causes an effect, and if you want to get better effects, you have to initiate the better cause.

This is the hard part, because we have to challenge our old habits of thinking and behavior, which we recognize need to be altered, and corrected. But our habits are set in concrete, are they not? This process usually is ongoing, because as we change, we alter our reactions, which in turn bring us different results, which cause us to have even more change. Hopefully this process is all for the better. But even when it backfires, at least you tried, and now you know what not to do, and you can try something else. Never give up, evaluate soundly, and just do it.

When you do something toward achieving your outcome, reward yourself with praise for at least attempting. Don't sabotage, try and do it better next time. Also if the goal is huge, break it down into smaller steps, and do something that is easier for you. As you get to each step, remind yourself of the times you handled this in the past, and just do it again. When you start to handle anything that has been an obstacle, you start empowering yourself with the belief you can overcome this, and you will, if you are persistent in your attitude.

Understanding feelings / emotions, is the crucial focus that I believe, has helped me personally. Learning that feelings, are simply feelings, which we choose to allow ourselves to experience from time to time. When we feel pain, for instance, (not physical pain, the other form), we are getting the message to change. We need to change our perceptions, or our procedures or both. Ask yourself "What else could this mean"? By doing this, you come up with empowering meanings to the event. This will allow you to regain control of your life, instead of having the event control you. When you go with the flow so to speak, which is what most of us do, we allow the miss interpretations of the events we experience, to lead us to create rules, beliefs, and set codes of conduct which restrict / limit, our growth to maturity.

I went to a "GROW" group (around 1998), after the suggestion of my psychiatrist, and was instantly attracted to their philosophy / psychology, as depicted in the literature. It was comforting to find an organization that existed which not only knew about mental health, but also had in place a method of overcoming problems of the mind. I soon found inner peace, within my own self, knowing that what I believed to be the truth, was actually shared by this group. And I was able to cope with the life I had chosen to lead, albeit in a marriage that was being kept together for the sake of our three children.

I have gained invaluable insight into myself, which I try to apply in every event. I realize that change can only be effected from within oneself. We might want others to change, and lead them to water, so to speak, but if they are not ready to drink?

I have still a long way to go. And I know that sometimes I'm going to screw up. But I also know where to go to seek help for myself now, in fact, after the death of my father, and some sleepless nights, I took myself to hospital, and was told I'm doing fine managing the situation myself. I am aware of how I'm feeling, and can take appropriate action myself. I don't allow the event to send me into the dark black hole of hopeless despair, and cause everyone to believe I'm "going around the bend", yet again.

During more recent events, I finally took the plunge and decided that I would grant the wish my wife was after for so long, a break. I have divorced her, and am picking up the pieces of my life once again. That was over ten years ago.

Now, that it is 2013, and this manuscript is within sight of seeing a printing press, I am happily continuing my journey through life, however with much greater ease and less trauma of the emotional rollercoaster ride experienced during the my first half century of living.

I am looking forward to a rewarding and full second half and beyond, GOD willing.

The things that I can say helped me are too numerous to go into detail. Suffice to say that even when it seemed hopeless, when everything fell apart, even when I was locked up, there was an inner strength. We all have it, I believe. I know what has happened to me, I don't pretend to know what is happening to you. All I know is that when the chips are down, you need to rely on your faith in GOD, a higher power, if you prefer. I would like to close with the following transcript, I am not the author, and I'm sure some of you have knowledge of it.

FOOTPRINTS

One night a man had a dream. He dreamed he was walking along the beach with the LORD. Across the sky flashed scenes from his life. For each scene, he noticed two sets of footprints in the sand: one belonging to him, and the other to the LORD.

When the last scene of his life flashed before him, he looked back at the footprints in the sand. He noticed that many times along the path of his life there was only one set of footprints. He also noticed that it happened at the very lowest and saddest time in his life.

This really bothered him and he questioned the LORD about it. "LORD, you said that once I decided to follow you, you'd walk with me all the way. But I have noticed that during the most troublesome times in my life, there is only one set of footprints. I don't understand why, when I needed you most, you would leave me?"

The LORD replied, "My son, my precious child, I love you and would never leave you. During your times of trial and suffering, when you see only one set of footprints, it was then, that I carried you."

CONCLUSION

Each one of us has the inner strength to face up to our life as it unfolds, and we all must rely on our faith alone, sometimes, to get us through any challenge that our circumstances bring to our table. NEVER give up your faith in GOD, or a higher power if you prefer. My story is just that, I'm sure you have heard others far worse. Yours, I'm sure is unique, as is everyone's. I for one, am proud to have had the experience and lived through all my trials and suffering. I believe I am more mature now, and like a fine brew, getting better with age. The best in life is yet to come, and whether or not it is clear to you, no doubt the universe is unfolding as it should.

My hope is that I can inspire someone else to learn to grow, their thinking, and develop into a more mature human being, and in so doing help other sufferers, through this journey called life. We all need to appreciate that whatever event is shaping our lives; it is the meanings we attach to it that controls our response. Is the meaning based on truth or just your imaginations or assumptions based on your beliefs that you have developed? Often we assume the worst, and react or over-react, when in fact if we examine carefully, using all the teachings found in the grow program, we can control our muscles to act in spite of our feelings.

GOD bless you all.

SUMMARY

There exists a life force.

You live your life in tune with this life force, your life will reflect your beliefs.

When you are out of SYNC with your life force, your life will be out of balance.

This out of balance can manifest itself in any of your three areas of yourself: body, mind and spirit.

Your overall good health must be taken as a complete package, not only in one area.

If you take control of your life force, you take control of your overall health in all three areas.

This manual explains this connection between the mind, body, and life force.

Simple PRINCIPLES can be mastered to achieve incredible life mastery skills.

These skills will affect any area you focus your attention on.

You can revolutionize your life if you follow these principals.

APPENDIX

The following are some affirmations that may remind yourself of who you really are . . . .

I AM

I AM A CHILD OF THE UNIVERSE.

I AM PART OF THIS UNIVERSE.

I AM CREATED IN GODS' IMAGE.

I AM CREATED FROM MY PARENTS.

I AM PART OF THEM.

I AM NO LESS IMPORTANT THAN ANYONE ELSE.

I AM A DROP IN THE OCEAN, A GRAIN OF SAND, &
    YET THESE WOULD BE LESS WITHOUT ME.

I AM WHATEVER I DECIDE TO BE.

I AM ABLE TO CHOOSE.

I AM ABLE TO TAKE ACTION.

I AM ABLE TO CREATE.

I AM ALL THAT I AM.

I AM THE WAY,

I AM THE TRUTH &

I AM THE LIGHT.

SOME THOUGHTS FROM A "GROW" GROUP IN AUSTRALIA.

WORRYING IS LIKE A ROCKING CHAIR. IT WILL GIVE YOU SOMETHING TO DO, BUT IT WON'T GET YOU ANYWHERE.

WORRY IS THE ADVANCED INTEREST YOU PAY ON PROBLEMS SELDOM COME.

KEEP IT AWFULLY SIMPLE OR IT MAY GET SIMPLY AWFUL.

BY ALWAYS SAVING FOR A RAINY DAY, WE MISS THE CHANCE TO DANCE IN THE SUN.

READING WITHOUT REFLECTING IS LIKE EATING WITHOUT DIGESTING.

SPEAK WHEN YOU ARE ANGRY, AND YOU WILL MAKE THE BEST SPEECH YOU'LL EVER REGRET.

TRUE FRIENDSHIP IS LIKE PHOSPHOROUS, IT GLOWS BEST AROUND YOU WHEN YOUR WORLD GETS DARK.

WHEN YOU THINK YOU HAVE REACHED THE END OF YOUR ROPE, TIE A KNOT AND HANG ON.

EVEN A MOSQUITO DOESN'T GET A SLAP ON THE BACK UNTIL IT STARTS TO WORK.

SOME PEOPLE ARE SO EAGER TO FIND FAULT, YOU'D THINK THERE IS A REWARD.

SOME PEOPLE ARE POOR LISTENERS BECAUSE IT INTERFERES WITH WHAT THEY WANT TO SAY.

SPEAKING WITHOUT THINKING IS LIKE SHOOTING WITHOUT AIMING.

NO MATTER HOW WELL WE NURSE THE RESENTMENT, IT NEVER GETS WELL.

RESENTMENTS ARE THE HEAVIEST WEIGHTS OF ALL TO CARRY.

IF YOU CAN'T LOOK ON THE BRIGHT SIDE OF LIFE, POLISH UP THE DULL SIDE.

EVEN IF YOU ARE ON THE RIGHT TRACK AND JUST SIT THERE, YOU ARE BOUND TO GET RUN OVER.

NO RECOVERY WILL WORK IF YOU DON'T.

HUG ME FROM BEHIND WHEN I'M CRANKY IN FRONT.

WE COME TO "GROW" TO GET A CHECK-UP FROM THE NECK UP.

DON'T JUST GO THRUGH PROBLEMS, GROW THROUGH THEM.

PRAYER OF SALVATION

OH GOD IN HEAVEN

I CALL UPON YOU IN PRAYER,

PLEASE FORGIVE ME MY SINS,

I BELIEVE JESUS CHRIST IS THE SON OF GOD,

I BELIEVE HE DIED ON THE CROSS FOR ME,

I BELIEVE HE ROSE FROM THE DEAD AND IS
ALIVE FOREVERMORE.

JESUS, PLEASE COME INTO MY HEART,

I RECEIVE YOU AS MY LORD AND SAVIOUR,

MAKE ME BRAND NEW IN EVERYTHING.

I WILL SERVE AND WORSHIP ONLY YOU,

FROM THIS MOMENT ON YOU ARE MY LORD.

I THANK YOU FOR YOUR SALVATION.

IN JESUS' NAME—AMEN.

THE SERENITY PRAYER

LORD, GRANT ME THE SERENITY TO ACCEPT THE THINGS I CANNOT CHANGE:

THE COURAGE TO CHANGE THE THINGS I CAN:

AND THE WISDOM TO KNOW THE DIFFERENCE.

WHAT NOW? . . . . Know, your TRUE self. To your own heart be true.

An organisation I have the utmost respect for is the Institute of HEART MATH. There you will find cutting edge research on the power your heart has in connecting with the FIELD. Many Tools and teachings that enable one to exercise greater awareness of this energy transceiver organ all life on planet Earth possesses. They also have a Global Coherence Initiative, which is monitoring the influence of the combined effect we have on the Earths' magnetic field. Fascinating research studies which indicate our connection and ability to sense this "feeling" is far greater than we currently know.

I am personally embarking on a new path in my own journey, having just attained certification as a REIKI 11 level healer, where this will lead me is exciting, to say the least.

I sincerely pray that you become aware of the infinite power and wisdom that each of you already have, in your spirit that resides within you, from the point of conception, throughout your advancing time on Earth, right up to the moment you draw your last breath, the spirit is there within you and then re-unites with itself and is forever expanding into the field of infinite possibilities.

I would love to receive your feedback and I invite you to send a friend request to:—Emiddio Joseph CATALDO, I will be actively posting interesting articles from cutting edge leading scientists and luminaries. Information that is already freely available.

You may send mailto: e.joecataldo@gmail.com or visit http://www.theuninhibitedmind.com/